# GAZZA'S FOOTBALL YEAR

## PAUL GASCOIGNE

### AND MEL STEIN

STANLEY PAUL

LONDON  SYDNEY  AUCKLAND  JOHANNESBURG

The photographs in this book
are reproduced by courtesy of
Action Images, AllSport, Colorsport,
Empics, Sporting Pictures (UK) Ltd,
and Bob Thomas

Stanley Paul & Co. Ltd
An imprint of the Random Century Group
20 Vauxhall Bridge Road, London SW1V 2SA

Random Century Australia (Pty) Ltd
20 Alfred Street, Milsons Point, Sydney, NSW 1061

Random Century New Zealand Limited
191 Archers Road, PO Box 40-086, Auckland 10

Century Hutchinson South Africa (Pty) Ltd
PO Box 337, Bergvlei 2012, South Africa

First published 1991

Set in Melior and designed by Brian Folkard Design

Printed and bound by
Scotprint Ltd., Musselburgh

A catalogue record for this book is available upon request
from the British Library

ISBN 0 09 174963 8

# Contents

# Acknowledgements

Our thanks go to Clare Tomlinson for her devoted research and interviews for the book and her patient picture editing, to Jayne Ball again for typing under pressure and to Cathy Phillips for her invaluable help when the going got tough. We'd also like to thank all the interviewees who gave their valuable time so willingly and hope we've accurately reported their views, and the photographers for allowing the use of copyright photographs.

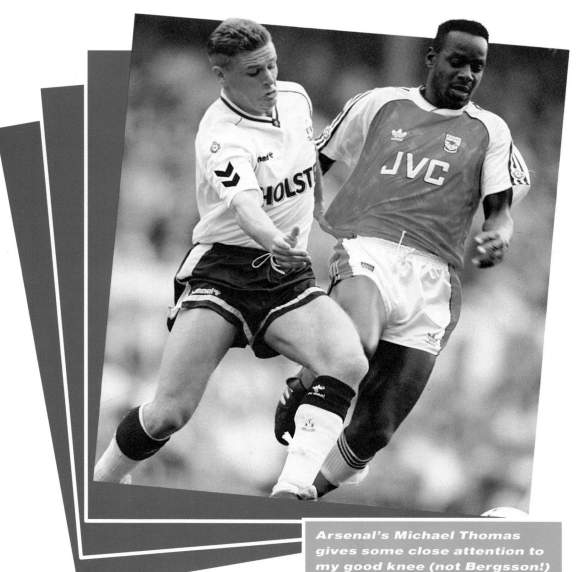

*Arsenal's Michael Thomas gives some close attention to my good knee (not Bergsson!)*

# *Introduction*

Who would have thought that a season which ended in Italy would be followed by a season full of speculation about me moving to Italy – yet instead saw me hobbling around on crutches? Who would have thought that a league season that saw Gary Lineker and I greeted as heroes in the August sunshine at White Hart Lane would see me carried off on a stretcher at Wembley on a dull May afternoon? Looking back now, that semi-final of the World Cup seems a long way away, a lifetime away, and perhaps it is. Some people say that Paul Gascoigne died and Gazza was born that night against West Germany, but they're wrong. Gazza has always been a part of me, Paul Gascoigne. Gazza and Gascoigne, it's not so much Jekyll and Hyde as is sometimes said, but more like Tweedledum and Tweedledee (only not so fat!). Without sounding bigheaded I can't think of anyone else in the world who has had a nickname that's stuck the way Gazza has stuck with me. Sure, you get pop singers like Sting whose real name is lost in the mists of history, but he gave himself that name. Gazza was given to me and I'll always be grateful for the gift.

It's hard in writing a book like this to decide where one season ends and another begins. Football's like that nowadays. The Football League says the season officially ends on the last full Saturday of the season. Yet most players' contracts run from the 1st July to the 30th June in any year. Then you've got the Cup Final in mid-May, the European Cup Final at the end of May, the play-offs spilling over into June, an England tour in the same month, and then it's back to pre-season training before the end of July. If I hadn't had my injury then I wouldn't exactly have had much time for a holiday. I had a meeting with Mel Stein, one of my business managers, at the Spurs training ground in early May this year to arrange for me to film a fishing video in June. 'What about a holiday?' I asked.
'That is your holiday,' he replied, 'sitting on the banks of the river doing nothing. Just forget the cameras and enjoy yourself!'

I finally negotiated myself, at that stage, two weeks away – two weeks after the sort of year I've had! It shows what a lousy negotiator I am, doesn't it? In fact my injury guaranteed me a really long holiday, although not one I was particularly looking for. Yes, it's been a really crazy year, not just on the pitch but off too. Sometimes people ask me, am I sorry it all happened, wouldn't I like to lead a normal life? I don't lead a normal life, but then I don't think I'm really a normal sort of person. Everybody who knows me will realise I can't sit still for more than five minutes without getting bored, and although some parts of 'Gazzamania' have got to me a bit I can honestly say I've not been bored this year. Even when I was in hospital after my hernia operation and recovering from my knee operation I kept busy at trying to get fit, setting myself targets even the doctors thought were impossible to reach. In fact it's all gone incredibly quickly.

It's not only goalkeepers who can catch a ball!

I was 23 years old on the 27th May 1990. I actually had two birthday celebrations, one with the England team when I can remember making a really long speech that had them booing me off when it turned into a list of my talents, and the other with the England side in Italy when a few reporters and the hotel got the date wrong – not like the press to make a mistake is it? That was the day which ended up with cake in my face courtesy of Chris Waddle. This year I 'celebrated' my twenty-fourth birthday at the Princess Grace Hospital, when there was a real chance that I would be throwing a party in Rome.

This book's about my year, *Gazza's Football Year*, a year that as far as I'm concerned started on the 4th July 1990 in Turin and came to an unpleasant halt on the 18th May 1991 at Wembley, a year that took me to Hungary and Ireland, a year that took me to Wembley, that had me meeting Mrs Thatcher and Princess Di, a year in which Princess Anne wanted to sell me, a year in which everybody wanted to sell me, a year which, in a way, never really ended at all.

# 1

# *Back from Italy*

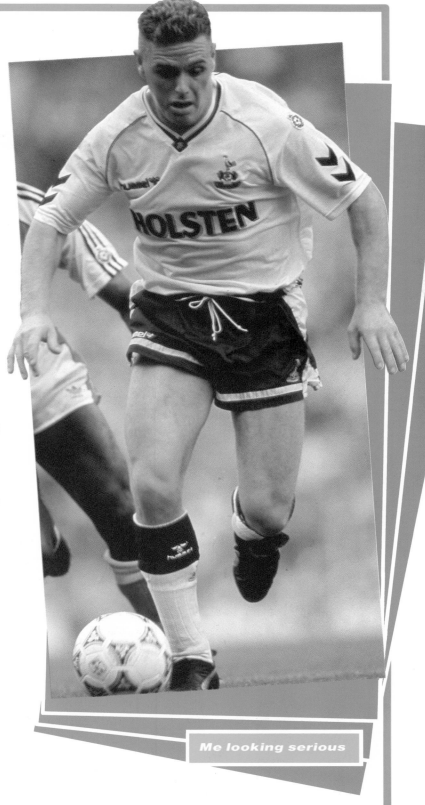

When I got back from Italy I went straight up to Newcastle with my Dad. He met me at the airport with his camper, Waddle and I were smuggled into the back and we slept all the way up the M1. It was lucky we did because it was the last good night's sleep I was going to have for a while.

My Dad took me to the Dunston Excelsior where the welcome was great, almost the best moment of Gazza's year. I'll never forget the warmth and support I got from the lads that night and I was able to bring a whole coachload of them down for the Cup semi-final against Arsenal, which is part of my way of saying 'thank-you'. Whatever else has happened this year, whenever I go back to Newcastle, and Dunston in particular, the blokes in the Club never let me forget who I really am — just a young fellow who's the son of John and Carol Gascoigne of Dunston, a lad who happens to play football a bit better than he plays darts.

*Me looking serious*

It was on the 13th July that it really began to strike home what was happening to me. Mel Stein and Len Lazarus came up to visit me and the three of us went out to dinner with Chris Waddle for Mel's birthday. He wouldn't say how old he was but he wasn't paying the fares on buses any more! Len told me that the phone hadn't stopped ringing and they needed to go through a few commercial possibilities with me. A few! It took nearly three hours to work our way through the list and by the time we were half-way done my head was spinning.

A new deal with the *Sun* newspaper, countless offers for a boot endorsement, T-shirts, games, a video biography, books, magazine articles, TV, radio, lunch boxes, duvet covers, curtains, poster magazines, prints, computer games. I couldn't believe it. It was only after the game at Wembley against Czechoslovakia that I really felt myself to be an England player, to be really part of the squad. That was on the 25th April. Now, less than three months later, I was some kind of national celebrity.

All the way through our meal at the Gosforth Park Hotel, people kept coming up to me and asking for autographs, Breakfast TV were begging me to appear the next day and incredibly enough the media had tracked us down and the phone didn't stop ringing. Mind you, every time Mel got up to answer the phone I took the opportunity to spike his champagne and orange juice. Despite that – or maybe because of it – he and Len managed to negotiate an interview with the *Mail on Sunday* for the following day at what appeared to me then to be a ludicrous fee, yet today is what I normally get paid.

Who says I don't talk to the Press?

The reporter and the photographer came down to my house and the Club the next day, and the bandwagon was beginning to roll. I've always been reported as saying I hate the press. That doesn't mean I hate individual journalists – most of the sports boys are decent lads who are trying to do a difficult job made more difficult by blokes like me. In fact, sports writers generally are a tired bunch of world-weary travellers who are a bit like a band of gypsies picking up their camps and setting them down again in different cities all over the world. You see them at the airports the day after an international match, bleary-eyed and hung-over, stories filed, rivalry put away, just chatting amongst themselves and to the players like any other football fans. Yet a few of them, it seemed to me then and seems to me now, were happy to let me be built up knowing

*Gary and me – one step nearer Wembley*

they were going to take the greatest pleasure in knocking me down. The news reporters were the worst. In those early days they hounded me and they hounded my family and friends. Anybody who'd ever met me – and some who'd only ever claimed to have met me – got interviewed. If I'd been in every place they said I was, with every girl they said was my girlfriend, done everything they claimed I'd done, I'd have been a burned-out, six-stone weakling in a month – if I'd lasted that long!

Yet there was a funny side to it. A school teacher brought all of his kids up to the front garden of my parents' house, knocked on the door and asked if I'd agree to have my photo taken. When I'm asked politely to do anything I never refuse but the garden was swarming with these kids and the photo session took ages. Everybody went away really happy until a few days later I got a note through my door asking if they could do it all over again as there'd been no film in the camera!

It was, I must admit, a bit difficult to turn my mind back to being a footballer; but that's what I was, that's what I am. I mentioned before the Gascoigne/Gazza relationship. I think it's too easy to say I'm Paul Gascoigne on the pitch and Gazza off it. The referees certainly don't distinguish between the two. Sometimes I think I'm being picked on because I'm Gazza but the name that goes in the book is always Gascoigne. Perhaps if I had two playing contracts, one in each name, I could divide the disciplinary points between them and get away without suspensions!

**Spurs squad 1990/91**

**Terry Venables – king of all he surveys**

Fortunately when I got back to Spurs for pre-season training it was not just me who'd been part of the England team. Gary Lineker had proved himself, in my view, an even bigger hero and success. It's always more difficult for a striker to stay at the top than a midfield player or defender. They rely on split second reactions and the fact that Gary has now played in two World Cups and is well on his way to a second European Championship shows what a great player he is. A few times this season the knives have been out for him but each time he comes back and answers his critics in the best possible way by finding the back of the net.

Obviously the rest of the Spurs team brought me down to earth very quickly. Every time I lost the ball in training they'd pretend to cry and ask me what deals I could get them! Terry Venables was, as always, very sympathetic. He'd been through it all when he'd gone to Spain and he took me aside and quickly warned me not to let it go to my head. In the playing sense he's done more than anybody for me. He's kept the media away from me at training, he's tried to make sure that I was just another player in the team, a part of a squad that was Tottenham Hotspur. He's had me concentrating on my game, improving certain techniques and attitudes, and even when he really needed me to play, when I was injured, it was always my decision as to whether or not I felt up to it. Sometimes it's been difficult for him to come to terms with the commercial demands on my time but he laid down certain ground rules and as long as we stuck to them he really didn't interfere. When my career finally takes me abroad it's Terry that I'll miss most, apart from my family.

But back in early August nobody dreamed I'd be anywhere else but White Hart Lane. Everybody felt that the 1991 season was going to be special, not just for Spurs but for

English football as a whole, and I think that proved to be right. The club's financial problems were just a little cloud on the horizon at that time, and although even then it was clear that there wasn't mega money around to buy new players the squad looked good enough on paper to win something. I must be honest and say that even in August I felt that we were going to be more of a Cup side than a team that would win the league. The league demands different qualities, and whilst I don't think Arsenal were a better team than Spurs, they were certainly a different sort of side and, as time proved, they were a different sort of side from Liverpool as well. Love them or hate them, for a team to go through a whole league season and lose only one match must prove something.

So when we all got together after the holidays (what holidays I ask myself – I did go away to Portugal for a few days but I was so bored I came back early) we were already on a high. Erik Thorstvedt in goal was getting better with every match. I've never seen a bloke practise so much; he even drives Ray Clemence mad with his insistence on being first out and last in. In defence we had Gary Mabbutt – team captain, who I thought was desperately unlucky not to be taken to Italy. I was really delighted when he got called into the England squad for the match against Turkey in May – if there's a better all-round defender in the English league I've yet to see him. Pat van den Hauwe has lost none of the battling qualities he'd shown at Everton – not the sort of bloke to meet down a dark alleyway, and with Steve Sedgley blinding the opposition with his good looks, Justin Edinburgh showing enormous promise after joining us from Southend, and the likes of Gudni Bergsson, Guy Butters, Terry Fenwick and Mitchell Thomas, the squad looked stronger at the back than it had done for years.

The midfield wasn't bad either, present company excluded. Paul 'Ollie' Allen was beginning to fulfill the promise shown at West Ham, Nayim was showing continental skills that sometimes went unappreciated – it took a while to explain to him that the crowd weren't barracking him when he got the ball, just giving the cockney version of his name – and then there was Vinny Samways. Vinny has been in and out of the team for a season or two, yet last season I think he really showed that he can produce the goods with the best of them. David Howells seemed willing and able to play anywhere. Then up front we had Gary Lineker, of course, now the England captain, with Paul Stewart and Paul Walsh, two strikers who'd waltz into most teams in the First Division.

Behind that main squad there were players like Paul Moran, my mate 'Sparrow', John Moncur, David Tuttle, Phil Gray, Ian Hendon, Peter Garland and Ian Walker, all of whom were to get a chance in the season to come. People may say that it was because there was no money to spend but Steve Sedgley, Pat van den Hauwe, Erik Thorstvedt, Gary Lineker and Nayim had all been relatively big money buys in the short time I'd been with the club, so who was to say that anybody else needed to be bought. All in all we looked forward to the first pre-season friendly with high hopes.

# 2
## Pre-season friendlies

I didn't actually play in the first couple of friendlies of the season against Ipswich and Maidstone but I did join up with the team in time for our tour of Ireland. Everybody knew I was coming and I was driven absolutely crazy by demands to make personal appearances and open stores while I was there. Regrettably I had to say no, not because I didn't want to do it but quite frankly I was worried about my own safety.

I'd come up against fans before, but the crowds in Ireland were something different. There were loads of young girls all screaming at me as if I were a pop idol. I was actually a bit frightened for them because I didn't think half of them had ever been to a football match before. The grounds at both Shelbourne and Derry were packed, the

Here the flags are out for the Republic, not for me!

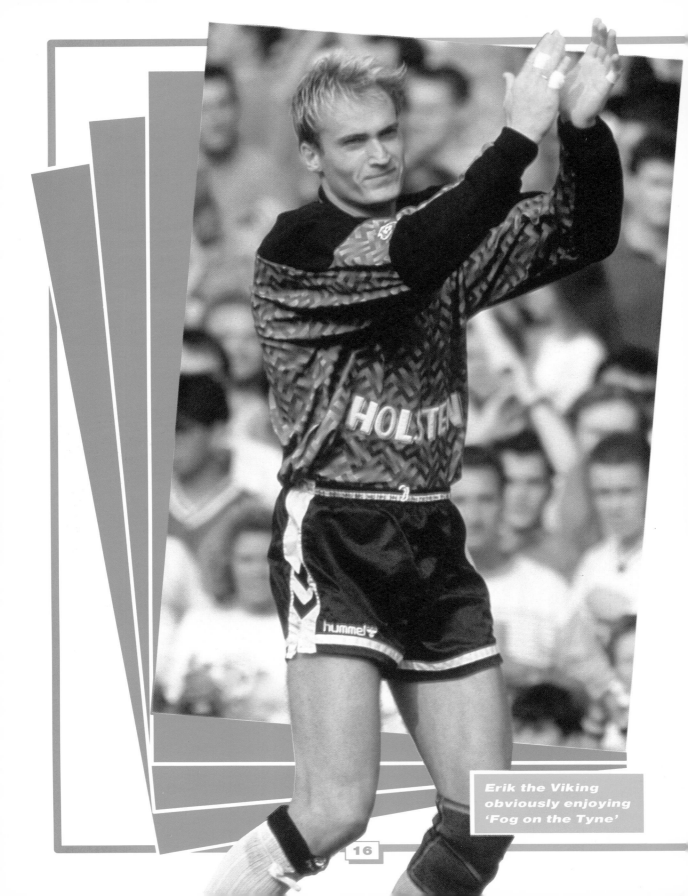

Erik the Viking
obviously enjoying
'Fog on the Tyne'

people literally hanging from the rafters and sitting in trees. The Irish are really lovely people, very warm and friendly and I felt almost as at home there as in the North East. I can understand why Roy Aitken was prepared to move from Newcastle United into Irish football at the tail-end of his career and I could also understand why the national team has been so successful. It's not just Jack Charlton and a bunch of nomads whose great grannies happen to have visited Dublin on an August Bank Holiday. It's a national identity carried along by a surge of passion that's really not seen outside of Newcastle or indeed Rome.

Anyway I scored twice against Shelbourne and felt really good. The World Cup had kept me sharp and fit and I'd not had a long enough lay-off to put on too much weight. We beat Derry 3–0 and although the opposition wasn't up to First Division standards we felt we were playing well as a team. From Ireland we went to Norway. I felt everything was going to be quieter there, but no such luck. The Norwegians have television and newspapers too, contrary to public opinion, and once again the teeny-boppers were out in their hundreds. We won against Brann 1–0 on the 7th August, drew with Viking 1–1, and beat the unpronounceable Sogndal 1–0.

Our Norwegian goalkeeper Erik, known officially as 'Erik the Viking' was in his element. The Norwegian language is totally incomprehensible – everybody sounds like the Swedish Chef from The Muppets and Erik, having been dubbed our official interpreter, may well have given his own version of what was said to us. I have the vague feeling that when I ordered steak I got a generous portion of reindeer (with a dash of Santa Claus on the side).

The Irish and the Norwegian trips were as much a way of re-establishing the team spirit as of getting us back to match fitness, and they did just the job. I was beginning to come to terms with the fact that my life had changed, that I couldn't just walk down the street any more; but on the other hand I didn't think it was going to last.

However, our match against Hearts left me under no illusions that my reputation had preceded me in Scotland as well. Again I needed protection to get into the ground but after the aggression I'd found at our pre-season friendly against Rangers the year before, the crowd this time were terrific. Tynecastle Park isn't a huge ground but it does hold 29,000 and for a pre-season friendly in August, when half of Scotland takes off for the coast, the crowd was enormous. They even had to delay the kick-off to let everybody in. By one of football's coincidences I found myself playing against John Robertson, who'd returned to Hearts from Newcastle. When I was negotiating with Newcastle before I moved to Spurs they'd just signed John and in fact the chairman Gordon McKeag had used that signing as an argument to demonstrate the club's ambition, feeling that John and I could have struck up a really good understanding. We never found out because I went to Spurs and after twelve games without scoring he returned to Hearts.

If you can't see me you can't book me!

The game finished 1–1; I came under the close scrutiny of the referee who booked me for smiling at him, but this was something I was going to get used to as the season wore on. People say I'm whingeing when I claim that referees pick on me. I don't think it can be denied that in the build-up to any game in which I play, my name crops up the most. That's not being bigheaded and believe me I wish it were otherwise, but it is a fact. Consequently, because of my profile all the referees know me by name and nature. Everything I do comes under scrutiny because the crowd are waiting for me to do something different, and if the crowd are watching and waiting so are the referees. If a player has a shock of red hair the ref'll notice him more than any other player on the field and I feel that if you're Gazza you also get more attention than anybody else. Some of the refs have been very understanding, accepting I've come under enormous pressure both on and off the field, but there are others who I feel have inflicted punishments on me which simply wouldn't have been doled out if my name was Fred Smith and I played for Hartlepool reserves. (I hope there's no-one at Hartlepool by that name otherwise he'll be in for a hard time with the men in black in future.) Some of the referees nowadays seem to be doing more interviews than the players. Yet if a player complains about a particular referee and a particular incident he can get into trouble with the FA. I've never seen a referee hauled up before a tribunal for talking about a player!

Although at times I accept I go over the top and deserve to be disciplined, it's only because I feel I have to play the game to win. Football's not a game for big girls' blouses. Nowadays I think referees give too much protection from the physical side of what is a physical game. Shoulder-to-shoulder charges seem to bring free-kicks as easily as vicious tackles from behind. I get criticised for using my arm to hold off players but I'm often only doing that because there's somebody pulling at my shirt and niggling at my ankles. The one thing that's been lacking this year is some consistency from the officials. That's been shown most clearly with regard to the 'professional foul'. Jimmy Case and Gary Pallister have had marching orders for tackles that were at worst clumsy whilst, even in Europe, Manchester United saw an opponent sent off in the final leg of the European Cup Winners' Cup semi-final for something that wasn't even a foul.

In order to cope with everything I'm all in favour of professional full-time referees. If you look at referees in a match you'll see they do every bit as much running as a midfield player, they get slaughtered by managers, players and the TV commentators alike, who have the benefit of action replays, yet all they get is a miserable few quid a match – it's almost like charity work. Have full-time refs who have time to train, time to get together during the week to discuss their approaches to matches, to review their own performances and the performances of their fellow refs on video and I guarantee you the English game will be much better for it.

Off the pitch Gazzamania was in full flow. I set up a fan club with my mum and sister

Lindsey running it up in Newcastle with the help of Sue and Linda of 'Star' down in London. In those early days the postman actually needed help with the mail which was coming in sackloads, not just from England but from every country you could imagine – there were enough foreign stamps to start a collection.

The *Sun* did a T-shirt offer which at the time broke all records for any offer they'd done on the paper, and still all the prospective licensees were lining up to sign me. It was very difficult because my basic instruction was not to let anything interfere with my football, but obviously the people who were going to produce 'Gazza' products wanted me personally to endorse them. In the end I think we managed to strike a very fair balance, and contrary to what the papers say I do very little promotional work considering how many products are on the market in my name. However I'm very careful to ensure that I don't agree to endorse any product that doesn't give value for money. We turned down hundreds of offers with which we didn't feel comfortable and I've virtually cut out all shop openings and appearances of that nature. In a mutual decision with Terry Venables, it was agreed I did nothing for forty-eight hours before any match of whatsoever nature. That rules out Thursdays and Fridays. Sundays I like to go back to my family if I can and if there's a mid-week match on a Wednesday then Mondays and Tuesdays are out as well – not much room for burn-out there.

*I was always faster than Stuart Pearce!*

I was particularly flattered when ITV's 'This Week' asked to make a documentary about me, although I thought it a bit unfair that they used a comparison of me and P. J. Proby – to be fair I'd never actually heard of him as he was a bit before my time, but seeing the state he's in has made me more determined than ever to succeed.

Everybody said I'd fail at Newcastle because I was a 'naughty boy'. Well, ask anybody on Tyneside whether or not I failed. Everybody said I'd be a £2 million flop at Spurs –

ask the faithful at White Hart Lane whether or not I've given them value for money. Everybody said Bobby Robson was taking a chance on picking me for England – ask the supporters who went to Italy who was right. Now everybody's written me off after my injury – well, given their success rate in prediction so far, who do you want to back?

Sorry – but I couldn't resist the dig. Anyway, back to August 1990. Even before the season started we'd got our commercial plans in order. 'Fog on the Tyne' was being recorded, 'Gazza – The Game' was in the pipeline. I'd finally signed a boot deal with Puma, new ranges of the Stuart Surridge balls were being developed and the shinguards were also on the market. We'd just started production of 'Gazza, the Real Me', my life story video, and negotiations were in hand with Brut for my product endorsement. My first computer game had already sold well and we agreed to do a second. A calendar was in production as was a picture biography and soccer skills book. Amongst all this was something which really upset me – an unauthorised biography written by Robin McGibbon. I've never met Mr McGibbon and how or why he feels qualified to write a book about me I don't know. I was already working on an authorised biography with Mel Stein which will be finished in a year or so. Maybe the people who co-operated with Robin McGibbon on his book thought it was the authorised one, maybe they just wanted to talk about me. Whichever it was, the book's full of inaccuracies which I'll correct in due course in my own book. Much was made of the court case to injunct him from using the name 'Gazza' and the performance of the judge who'd never heard of me. I wonder if he's heard of me now?! He even got his operas mixed up. After my concentrated efforts to learn Italian at least I know that 'La Gazza Ladra' is 'The Thieving Magpie' – not a bad description really!

On the 17th August we played Ray Clemence's benefit match against West Ham and won 4–1 (not a bad result seeing how the Hammers have done this season) and then wound up with a 4–1 win against Justin Edinburgh's Southend on the 20th August. Southend also won promotion so maybe more teams should line up to play Spurs in pre-season friendlies.

But as 25th August approached it was time to face up to the real thing, to push everything else aside. Whatever I was earning off the field, whatever I'd done in the World Cup, that would all come to nothing if I couldn't reproduce my summer form on the field in the English First Division.

# Early season

Saturday 25th August 1990 was cricket weather. The crowd were in shirt sleeves and as we sweated during the warm-up I thought I was back in Italy.

Manchester City were our first opponents, still re-establishing themselves in the First Division, and with a new manager in Howard Kendall just back from his foreign exploits. Nobody knew then that before the season was over he'd be back at Everton where his career had first taken off. Meanwhile, as he's done right through his managerial career, he'd gathered around him players with

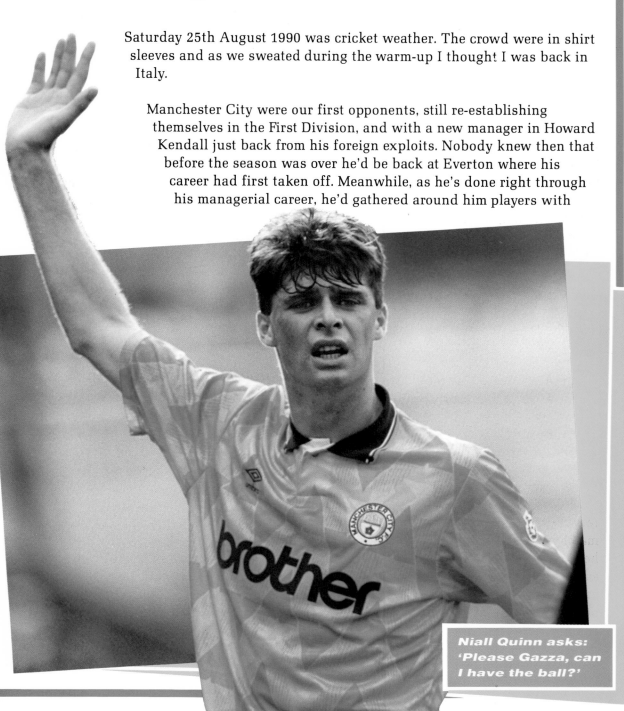

*Niall Quinn asks: 'Please Gazza, can I have the ball?'*

*Clive Allen giving Spurs the lead against Coventry in the '87 Cup Final. Unfortunately they didn't keep it...*

whom he felt comfortable. Alan Harper, Gary Megson, Mark Ward, Wayne Clarke and Adrian Heath had all spent some time at Everton and he'd added the height and awkwardness of Niall Quinn up front. Niall scored an equaliser for City that day, the first of many goals he was to score in a wonderful season.

It says a lot for George Graham that having sold a player of Niall's quality he then won the championship for Arsenal using very able players such as Alan Smith and others with exciting potential such as Paul Merson and Kevin Campbell. Niall not only had a great season for City but he didn't do too badly for Eire either and in many people's eyes he was in contention for the Player of the Year Award — he certainly had to be considered as the most improved player of the year. City had another Tottenham favourite in the shape of Clive Allen, back from Bordeaux, although he spent a lot of matches on the substitutes' bench, never recapturing the incredible goal-scoring form he showed with Spurs, 60 goals in only 105 appearances. Chris Waddle always used to say he was the best scorer of goals at the near post he'd ever seen. Near-post scoring is an art in itself and is in a way much more difficult than any other method of getting the ball into the back of the net. You need split second reactions, great timing and courage to get in there where the feet and the fists are flying.

The match was played in a real carnival atmosphere. There was a big 'Welcome Back' sign hung across the entrance to the ground for Gary and I, and we were both very touched by the way the Spurs fans saw us as representing Tottenham for England, and England for them. I've not explained that very well – it's the sort of thing you have to feel rather than say but everybody who's cheered for me, either in a Spurs or England shirt, will know exactly what I mean. Inside, the ground was packed. Gary Lineker put Spurs ahead before Niall equalised and then Gary got another and I got one to set us off to a flying start with a 3–1 victory. The crowd was over 33,500 that day and it says a lot for the resilience and entertainment value of Spurs that it was not until we played Southampton in April, when we'd long given up any hopes of the championship, that the gate fell for the first time below 25,000.

The headlines the next day were all about World Cup duos but the win was a team effort and as a team we had to go back up to the North East for our next match away to Sunderland. Sunderland's rise to the First Division had been very controversial. It was actually Swindon who'd won the play-offs but when they were demoted after that financial scandal there was a strong argument that Newcastle should have gone up as they'd finished six points clear of Sunderland; but it wasn't to be and it was their deadly rivals who got the vote. It wasn't that clear when they held us 0–0 in August that they were going to struggle, but giving the performances of the ageing Newcastle side in the Second Division (at least until Ossie Ardiles came in and gave the kids a chance) I think the Geordies would have found it even harder.

My reception at Sunderland was more chaotic than anything I'd experienced before. I had to be taken out of the ground in the boot of a car – something else I was going to get used to as the season wore on. The one thing I don't go to on principle is car boot sales – one day I'm going to write a book

**Kieron Brady, North East star of the future**

**Paul Davis with his elegant left foot**

about the inside of car boots and give some tips to the designers on how to make them more comfortable.

There's no doubt Sunderland have some promising players. Kieron Brady is one of my tips for the top and I still don't think Marco Gabbiadini has yet shown his full talents. He's got incredible pace and with a bit more discipline in his shooting he must be pushing for England honours in the next few years – can you imagine a Gabbiadini leading the England attack against Italy! I was also delighted to face up to Paul Bracewell even though he gave me a hard time. His career has been terribly interrupted by injuries and there's no doubt in my mind that if he hadn't had such bad luck he'd be one of the players I'd be struggling to replace in the England team. As it is I have enormous sympathy with him given my fight back to fitness. He had a very good game against us that night and continued to play well all season as everybody saw when Sunderland held Arsenal to a goalless draw in May's televised match.

On the 1st September we were back home, but away. That means a match at Highbury. Nobody on either side actually enjoys a North London derby and generally speaking they're not very good matches. The FA Cup semi-final later in the season was an exception but this one wasn't. It was niggly from the start, not helped by the fact that the press were claiming I was tired by all my off-the-field activities. That was nonsense. If I was tired it was because I'd had no real rest from football. I'd had a long, hard season with Spurs, then gone on tour with England, off to Italy, back to Ireland and Norway and then played three tough matches in six days. Who wouldn't be tired? We didn't take a conscious decision then, or afterwards, to cut down on commercial activities because, as I've said, my involvement was minimal.

The other unfair aspect of the build-up to the Arsenal game was the comparisons between myself and the Arsenal midfield trio of Paul Davis, David Rocastle and Micky Thomas. We're all different players and I have the greatest respect for all of them. Paul Davis, in particular, had a super season and there were signs at the end of the season that 'Rocky' Rocastle is also coming back into favour. I really hate seeing in the newspapers side-by-side analysis of two teams with points out of ten given to each player. Every player's performance is for ninety minutes of that particular match and what they've done before or will do again is irrelevant. Still, I suppose the press have to find some way to fill their pages when they've nothing sensational to write about. The Arsenal game finished 0–0 and we thought perhaps the first rush of goals was

drying up. However, back at White Hart Lane we faced Derby whose miserable season was just beginning. I felt desperately sorry for Arthur Cox who found himself in the same position as Terry Venables in that he was without money to spend, but perhaps had a less talented squad despite the presence of fine individual players in the shape of Dean Saunders, Mark Wright and Peter Shilton.

To score a hat-trick against Peter is like scoring ten against any other 'keeper. Without being cruel, I just loved the look on his face when my first free kick went in

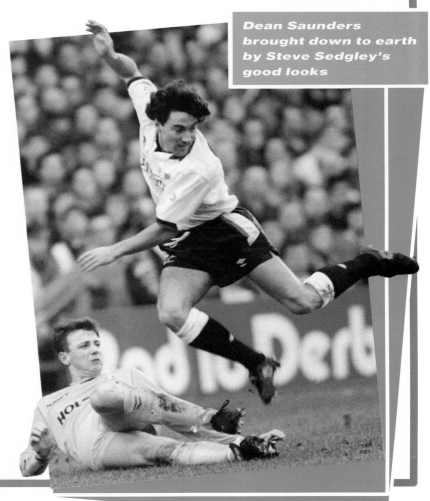

*Dean Saunders brought down to earth by Steve Sedgley's good looks*

and the expression of disbelief when I did it again when he'd obviously convinced himself I couldn't. Although Derby have gone down, their 6–2 thrashing of Southampton in the last but one game shows that they'll be back, although I can't see some of their more talented players hanging around in the Second Division for too long. So, another 3–0 win, four matches played, six goals scored (four by me) only one conceded and things couldn't have started better.

The other thing was that we'd started each match with the same eleven players – unkind people might say that was because we didn't have anybody else, but when you see that our substitutes had been Paul Walsh and Vinny Samways that was obviously untrue. The Italian summer was turning into a very pleasant English autumn.

*On my way to a hat-trick against Derby*

# 4

## Autumn fixtures

**David Howells after breaking the Gazza/Gary scoring monopoly against Leeds**

They give nowt away at Leeds, yet on the 15th September we went there and came away with a 2–0 win. Gary Lineker again, but this time David Howells scored the first non-Gazza/Gary goal of the season. You have to look at results with hindsight and beating a relegated Derby 3–0 at home may not have meant much, but Leeds finished fourth, while Palace our next opponents finished third. I scored again against Palace (yes I know it's getting boring) in a 1–1 draw and we'd now played six matches undefeated, including games against three teams who were to finish in the top four. I'd scored five goals and felt confident enough to take Glen Roeder on for a bet that I'd top 20 for the season. You may think the operation I had was because of an injury but actually I think Roeder bribed the doctors to operate in order to avoid having to pay me off on the bet.

We were drawn against Hartlepool in the Rumbelows Cup and I looked forward to playing against my old friend Joe Allon. Joe was Hartlepool's top scorer last season when they gained promotion from the Fourth Division rather than struggling against relegation to the Conference. It's really quite amazing that he's been made the North East Player of the Year, an award that usually goes to someone who plays for one of the big three clubs in the area. In fact with Darlington also coming up, the so-called 'big three' will have to be on their toes. I've always said that Joe was too good a player to stay in the Fourth Division. Cyril Knowles worked wonders up there – 'Nice one, Cyril.' It's so cruel that his managerial career has been cut short by illness. There doesn't seem to be too much room for sentiment in the game nowadays.

Fortunately for Spurs, Joe didn't turn it on against us and although we were slightly flattered by the scoreline of 5–0 I did score four goals to bring my tally to nine in seven matches. Roeder was shaking in his shoes, getting ready to pawn the family's silver.

Aston Villa, Taylorless but under the new (and now old) manager Jozef Venglos, (sounds a bit like a foreign spy to me, that one) were next and we beat them 2–1 with goals from Paul Allen and Gary Lineker, his fifth of the season. I don't think he really fancied being out-scored by a midfielder. This match was memorable for a horrible incident when David Howells went up for a ball with Gary Mabbutt and there was a clash of heads. David went down and he swallowed his tongue and it was down to Dave Butler, the Tottenham physiotherapist, to save his life. We all felt helpless just standing around and I think there's a lot to be said for the players themselves having compulsory first aid lessons. David Platt had a really good game against us, as did Tony Daley (despite his haircut); I don't understand these young players who feel the need to have outrageous hairstyles!

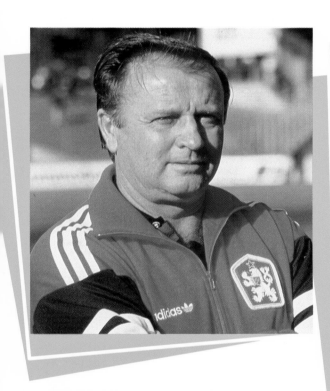

*Left: Joe Allon in champagne mood after Hartlepool clinch promotion against Northampton*
*Above: Jozef, are you Big Ron in disguise?*
*Right: Can I give you the name of my barber, Tony?*

After eight matches we'd had only one team change, Edinburgh for Bergsson against Hartlepool and in the league there'd been no changes at all. I'm a great believer in keeping the same team. If you think they're good enough in the first place why not give them time to get it right? If ever I'm a manager one of the things I'll show is patience in team selection (do I hear laughter at me describing myself as patient?!)

I was a bit disappointed by a goalless draw at QPR. I thought we'd done enough to win, but not only were we still unbeaten after nine matches, but we'd only conceded three goals in the league – not bad for a defence that was regarded as suspect at the start of the season. Paul Parker had a smashing game against us; it was a shame that his season also had to be disrupted by injury. I got myself booked for arguing with Mr Pierce the referee.

With a 5–0 lead from the home leg against Hartlepool, we could afford to take chances and to give me a rest I was named only as a substitute against them in the second leg in the North East. Even so, I got a big cheer when I came on. While I was sitting on the bench I had a bit of fun with the ball-boys and as I warmed up I told them to copy me doing press-ups, then when they weren't looking I walked away leaving them to it. Some of them may still be there today! I really enjoyed the welcome I was given in the North East. Although the madness of August had died down a bit I was still amazed by my personal following and by the fact that whatever I did was news. This book's mainly about football but I have to report that I couldn't even talk to a girl without being married off to her. We ran out 2–1 winners, 7–1 on aggregate, and Paul Stewart finally broke the ice for the season. He'd been getting a bit of stick, quite unfairly, because his work rate had been phenomenal, and with his temperament which had got him into so much trouble the previous season properly controlled, it was his efforts up front that gave Gary and I so much freedom.

Sheffield United, Vinnie Jones and all, were next on the agenda. If you remember, they were on the most dreadful run and looked as if they'd be relegated by Christmas, until an incredible revival took them to a respectable position. We did nothing for them, and in a 4–0 win I was substituted. I'd been feeling my groin injury all season; the aching actually started in Italy, and if I had to pick a match where I knew in my heart of hearts something was wrong I suppose this was it. Still, bottom club for opposition or not, you can't do much more than win 4–0. I must confess to having been a bit knackered as I'd played for England against Poland just three days earlier. I've talked about the England season in a different chapter but there's no doubt that 90 minutes at Wembley takes more out of you than any other pitch in the world. We didn't really see Sheffield United at their best (and indeed they were reduced to ten men after sixty-four minutes when Barnes was sent off) although I did think that Tony Agana up front looked more than useful.

Although we obviously didn't know it at the time, the 27th October was a Cup Final

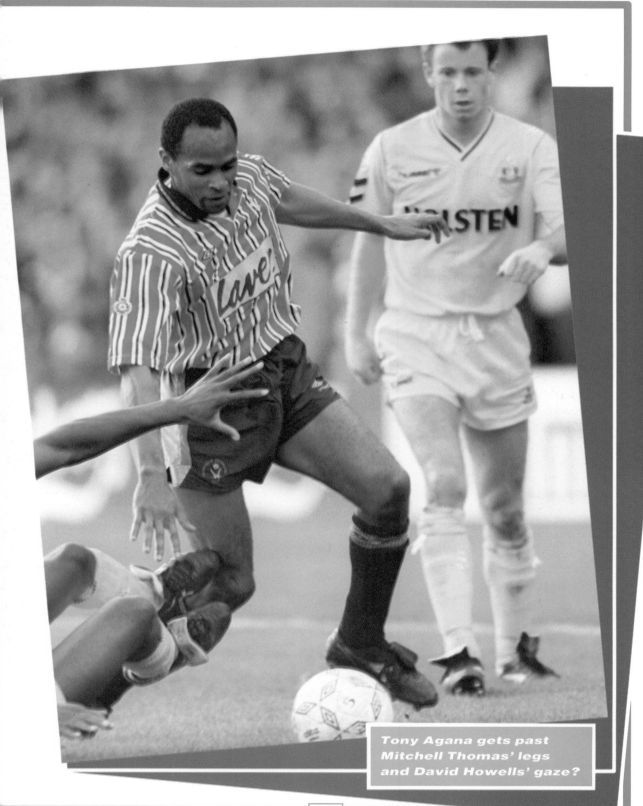

Tony Agana gets past
Mitchell Thomas' legs
and David Howells' gaze?

rehearsal and with David Howells scoring twice it was to be a big psychological boost looking back before Wembley to know that we'd actually won 2–1 at Forest.

Nigel Clough put Forest ahead after 16 minutes, and David's goals came in the 68th and 90th minutes. This was the first time I'd played against Roy Keane and I thought he was really tricky. Clough's goal was actually the first goal we'd conceded away from home all season.

Bradford City were our next opponents in the Rumbelows Cup, and after a brief scare when we were a goal down we ran out 2–1 winners with Stewey scoring again and me getting into double figures and putting more pressure on Roeder.

Everything was perfectly set for a televised fixture against Liverpool who were also unbeaten. Personally, I hate Sunday matches. It just doesn't feel right playing any time except Saturday afternoons or on a mid-week evening. I like to be with my family on Sundays and apart from the Cup semi-final (which at least had a civilised kick-off time of noon) my record on televised Sunday matches is appalling. Alright I know that on the Continent most matches are on Sunday....

Everybody was billing this one as a Championship decider – crazy in November with less than a third of the season gone, but I hate to admit, it did actually get to the lads

**Gudni Bergsson getting trampled in the 'Rush' against Liverpool**

and me in particular. I was incredibly wound up before the match, and Kenny Dalglish was a shrewd enough manager to pick his team accordingly. He put David Burrows out to mark me and it has to be said he did a very good job. Although Gary Lineker scored we went down 3–1, and not only was that good-bye to our unbeaten record but if you'd asked me at that moment who'd win the league I would have said that Liverpool were certainties.

We came bouncing back in a big way the following week when we beat Wimbledon 4–2 at White Hart Lane. A lot's been written about Wimbledon's style but you have to give them credit. Less than ten years ago they were

I'm Keith, fly me. Paul Allen gets on board Keith Curle's back

in the same position as Barnet, a little London club who'd just come into the league with a small unsightly ground and even smaller hardcore of supporters. In that time they've not only got to the First Division, but they've actually stayed there and won the Cup, and last season in particular they played a fair bit of good football. Graham Taylor's realised that too and there's been well deserved international recognition at one level or another for Roger Joseph, John Fashanu and Keith Curle. I always think it's smashing when someone like Keith Curle has some success (although it was terrible luck breaking his jaw in Australia – that's what you get just for talking to David Batty!). He's 27 years old and had played over two hundred games with Bristol Rovers, Torquay, Bristol City and Reading before joining Wimbledon. None of them are exactly so-called fashionable clubs, none of them are talked about in terms of a super league, and that must be a prime example of why the super league is a lousy idea. All we'd get would be the same as happens in Scotland, the same teams playing each other week in and week out, the odd team coming into the Premier Division, finding the pace too hot to handle and going out again, the honours always with the same few clubs. For me football's as much about Hartlepool playing Darlington as Arsenal playing Spurs. That's what makes our league the most fascinating in the world and there's no point in messing with it.

# The winter sets in

The TV cameras must have liked what they saw against Liverpool even if we didn't because they had us on again against Everton on Sunday 18th November. Everton were having a terrible time of it. They were two from bottom while their great Merseyside rivals were six points clear at the top and actually twenty-six points clear of Everton – an incredible gap after only fourteen matches. It didn't surprise me that Howard Kendall looked like he was turning it around at the end of the season – they finally finished a respectable twelfth – but what did surprise me was that my old friend Neil McDonald fell out of favour. Whenever I saw Neil play last season he looked Everton's best player, and he actually had a very good game against us, very nearly scoring. He's one of those uncomplaining players who gets shifted around from position to position just because he can play in every position. He left Newcastle because of that and now he's suffering the same fate. He actually played with me in the England Under-21 side, and I've always been a bit surprised that he and Gary Porter from Watford aren't playing for the full senior team.

Anyway, back in November, Everton had a real go and went 1–0 up through Stuart McCall, another fiery midfielder for whom I've a lot of respect. David Howells equalised just before half time and that was how it finished. We were still third in the league, three points behind Arsenal, who to be fair had suffered the deduction of two points arising from the Manchester United incident. Personally I thought that was blown out of all proportion. Obviously you shouldn't argue with the referee and if you do you risk the consequences, namely a booking or a sending-off – believe me I know that more than most – but to take it further and punish a whole team and its supporters for one incident in what is a very tense and stressful season in my opinion just isn't fair. One of the players who came out of it the worst was poor Paul Davis. Several papers said he'd been seen to throw a punch. The word 'punch' gave them a hook (get the joke!) relating to the Glen Cockerill incident a few seasons ago. This time Paul didn't punch anybody and the *Mirror* actually had the grace to apologise.

Back home against Norwich the following week we won 2–1. Gary Lineker was back in scoring touch, putting the ball home from close range after Paul Stewart had headed down. Just another example of Stewey's unsung contribution to the side this year even before he moved back so successfully into midfield. Norwich were full of ex-Tottenham players, Culverhouse, Bowen and Crook, an amazing coincidence that so many young ex-Spurs players should turn up in one team. It was one of them, Ian Crook, who scored with a 25-yard free kick just to prove that I'm not the only one who can do it.

If you said excuse me, Stewey still wouldn't let you through

You always find that when a player comes up against his old side he's trying to do something special. It was a great shame when Newcastle dropped out of the First Division because I always enjoyed the challenge of going back to St James's Park. Gary Lineker got our winner that day to bring his tally to nine and with me having scored ten he was breathing down my neck.

Although I didn't pay a lot of attention at the time, in Italy a little team called Lazio were only five points behind Sampdoria at the top and like us they'd also only lost one match – mind you they had drawn six out of the nine they'd played!

**Walshy and I jumping
for joy after he scored
against Sunderland**

We saw Sheffield United off fairly easily in the fourth round of the Rumbelows, 2–0, with Stewey and I scoring. I edged a bit further ahead of Gary in the goal stakes. With one defeat in eighteen matches we were still feeling pretty confident about things and as we'd only used fifteen players there was a nice tight-knit feeling about the squad.

December, though, was a disaster. Chelsea, who were to be our jinx team all season (mind you, they didn't do too badly against Arsenal and Liverpool either) beat us 3–2. They were 2–0 up at half time with goals from Dixon and Bumstead. I pulled one back, they went 3–1 up through Durie, Gary missed a penalty and then scored nine minutes from the end for some consolation. To be fair, we only really played in the second half and if you don't play for ninety minutes you can't complain if you don't win. The result was disappointing but we'd still only lost two in the league and that was Championship form.

A home game against a struggling Sunderland faced us but as so often proves the case we were over-confident and went 2–0 down by half time. Super-sub Paul Walsh pulled us back to 2–2 and just as we looked like getting on top and earning three points, Sunderland scored through Colin Pascoe. You could hear the old familiar sound of seats being lifted when Gary got an equaliser dead on time. Oh, by the way, I got booked. I can't actually remember which of the referees took my name but I had a bit of a choice! Mr Ashby should have taken control of the match but got stuck in Worcester because of bad weather. Mr Hemley took over and then had to go off himself with a thigh strain. The senior linesman, Mr Alexander, finally finished the match. There's one for the quiz books!

*Shall we dance?! The invitation's extended by Carl Bradshaw of Sheffield United*

We were still third, not only eight points behind Liverpool but also six points behind Arsenal. The gap was widening. Sheffield United at this stage had only four points from fifteen matches, and were eight points behind Queen's Park Rangers. When you consider the Blades' recovery, which I've already mentioned, and the fact that QPR finished just behind us, it makes you wonder whether or not we could have had a QPR/Sheffield United challenge for the title if they'd both started the season properly.

I scored what I thought was a pretty good goal at Maine Road against Manchester City but it didn't do us a lot of good because we still lost 2–1, conceding both goals, one a penalty, in the last fourteen minutes. It's amazing how often a home team can trail for most of the match and then come back late on to win, spurred on by the crowd. Even less happy for me was the fact that I got booked again, although this time I had company in the referee's book in the shape of Nayim and David Howells.

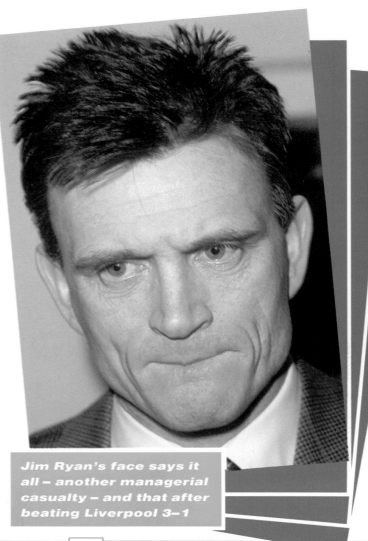

We did beat Luton 2–1 just before Christmas, although again we went a goal down before Stewey scored twice. Luton aren't the same side away from the artificial pitch and it'll be interesting to see how they get on when they have to play home and away on real grass. I must say I think Jim Ryan, their manager, was a bit hard done by to get the sack after he'd kept them up two seasons running. OK – it went to the last game each time, but meanwhile they've played First Division football on limited means while so-called moneybag clubs like Sheffield Wednesday and Sunderland have been relegated. I heard that Sheffield Wednesday had more insurance on Ron Atkinson's jewellery than

Jim Ryan's face says it all – another managerial casualty – and that after beating Liverpool 3–1

*The enigmatic Matt le Tissier loses out this time to Gary Mabbutt*

Luton had on their entire team! That's only a joke, honest. I really rate Luton's Kingsley Black, the young Irish winger, and David Preece always gives me a hard battle in midfield.

Unlike some teams, we didn't have a match on the Saturday before Christmas but our away game on Boxing Day against Coventry was hardly worth waiting for. Goalless at half time, I think it was our worst display of the season and probably the worst match after the Arsenal 0–0 draw. It got worse when Gallacher scored just after half time and Gynn added a second and we went home to look at our cold turkey and try to work out why we'd only won one of our last six matches. Some people say that titles are won and lost at Easter but I always think that Christmas is much more of a pointer to how the season will end. Somehow or other you seem to take a deep breath at the end of the year and if you're on a roll it's just that much easier to carry on the momentum into the New Year.

Things went from bad to worse for us against Southampton on the 29th December. I've always rated Matthew Le Tissier. There was a strong rumour that he was joining Spurs last season and I would have loved to have had the chance of playing alongside him. He actually reminds me of Chris Waddle, tall, gangly, looking a bit awkward if not permanently knackered off the ball. But once he gets the ball and gets up a bit of steam he's virtually unstoppable. He's got incredible balance and also has the same trick as Chris of dropping his shoulder and going past his man either on the inside or the outside. I missed this match as my groin was playing me up but he took us apart, scored twice, and we lost 3–0. It was the first league match I'd missed and there's nothing worse than having to sit a game out when you're injured and seeing your team lose. You just feel helpless and frustrated.

All that frustration came to the boil on New Year's Day against Manchester United. I think everybody who saw that game on TV will acknowledge we were the better team. Yet I got myself sent off and we lost. I've apologised in public and through the press and I'll do it again. Whether or not I agree with the referee's decision I should never have put him in the position where he had the choice of making that decision. Yes, I swore, but at myself not at him. On a strict interpretation of the law that's an offence. I know a lot of kids will read this book and I'm always careful to control my language in front of children. Believe me sometimes when I hear the obscene chanting that comes from the terraces I get really embarrassed for the kids in the crowd. But most referees do tolerate a bit of language on the field. It's a man's game and it can get rough and tough. I bet language on a football field is nothing compared to what goes on at rugby matches and you rarely see any rugby player penalised for swearing. Still, at 1–1 after sixty-six minutes with us pressing for the winner I do have to accept that my dismissal probably handed Manchester United the three points on a plate. You can't point to any one match and say 'That's when our Championship challenge ended', but there's no doubt that the defeat against United, bringing up a run of one win in seven, saw us drop out of serious contention.

Not only that but I had a suspension to look forward to. 1991 had started no better than 1990 had ended and I wasn't to know then that there was even worse to come.

# 6

## 1991 and all that

Suspensions don't start immediately and I was left to look forward to the prospect of having to face the 'friendly' taunts of the Arsenal fans in the reverse fixture at White Hart Lane. Arsenal were by now really pushing for the title while our awful run and the news of the financial problems off the pitch did little for our confidence. Terry Fenwick made his comeback from yet another dreadful injury in this match and did really well. Some players (me included it seems) are just dogged by bad luck when it comes to injuries. Bryan Robson and Terry Fenwick are examples. If there's such a thing as slaughtering the other team in a 0–0 draw we did it that day. We did everything but score and it was no coincidence that every newspaper had David Seaman as their man of the match. Thank goodness he didn't play like that against us in the semi-final.

Just four days later we had to face Chelsea in what looked to

*It helps if you're facing the goal, Stewey – Dave Seaman takes another clean catch*

A unique photo – Arthur Cox smiling – but then Derby have beaten Plymouth 4–2

be a difficult fifth-round Rumbelows Cup-tie at Stamford Bridge. Chelsea had beaten us once in the league and were just two points behind us. It was a pressure match and a terrible time for my two-match suspension to start. Yet we went there, battled, and got a goalless draw. We thought we'd done the difficult bit and I was looking forward to playing in the replay.

Before that happened we travelled to Derby and I was, to say the least, disappointed not to be playing against Arthur Cox's team. It says a lot for Arthur's talents and the respect in which he's held that, although Derby were relegated, nobody blamed him and indeed he seemed destined for greater things in the game. Vinny Samways, who'd been incredibly patient all season, came in to play in my place and did really well in a televised 1–0 win. I'm sure both Arthur and Derby will be back.

It was becoming clearer and clearer that our real hope of winning something lay with one of the Cup competitions and I was pleased to be back from my suspension for the Rumbelows Cup replay against Chelsea – at least I thought I was pleased until we got tonked 3–0. We didn't even start to play that night as Terry Venables later told us in no uncertain terms and it was all the more upsetting having gone to Stamford Bridge and got a draw. So we were out of the title race, out of the Rumbelows and that just left the FA Cup. I've devoted a whole chapter to the FA Cup!

By this stage in the season I was in a bit of trouble with my groin. My friends the Press got hold of what they thought was a major story and every time I went off to a health club I was supposed to be disappearing to a private clinic either for an operation or for treatment. One of the papers even suggested I had a drink problem and I'd gone away to dry out!

My old mate Chris Waddle had experienced a double hernia operation a couple of years ago and what he'd told me about it terrified me. If there are two things in life that really scare me, they are flying and doctors – no prizes for guessing my least favourite TV programme – yes 'Flying Doctors'. So it didn't need a lot of persuasion to put me off an operation and the game plan from a very early stage in the season was to coax me through, with any operation I might need taking place at the end of the season. I was assured by the specialist that it wasn't dangerous for me to play, but I

'There's someone behind you Ollie.' Paul Allen seems oblivious to Tony Dorigo (then of Chelsea) in the Rumbelows Cup

must tell you now that at times it wasn't half painful. Some of my critics sometimes have a go at my attitude and commitment to the game. Without claiming to be a hero I'd really like them to try and go through what I had to put up with between Christmas and March.

The general approach was that I'd keep match fit by training as hard as it was safe to do, play part of the odd league match to sharpen up my game and then really go for it in the Cup, with the help of pain-killing injections.

So I missed a goalless draw against Leeds in early February and very fortunately missed a 5–1 drubbing by Wimbledon at Plough Lane, where my good mate Gudni Bergsson got the one consolation goal. If this has not been the greatest year for me (what with operations, bookings, sendings-off and all those months of rehabilitation) it's been quite awful for Gudni. He came to Spurs not long after me as an Icelandic international, but whilst by the Cup Final I'd played well over 100 times for the club, Gudni had only made 35 league appearances. He'd started the season in the regular right-back slot and had played in seven opening league games in which we were unbeaten. Yet between February and April (when he came on as a sub against Sheffield United) he spent his time in the reserves. It's interesting that he has always said his best position is sweeper and that's where he played very successfully in the combination team that lost only one game in his time with them. I just hope he gets a chance, either with Spurs or some other club,

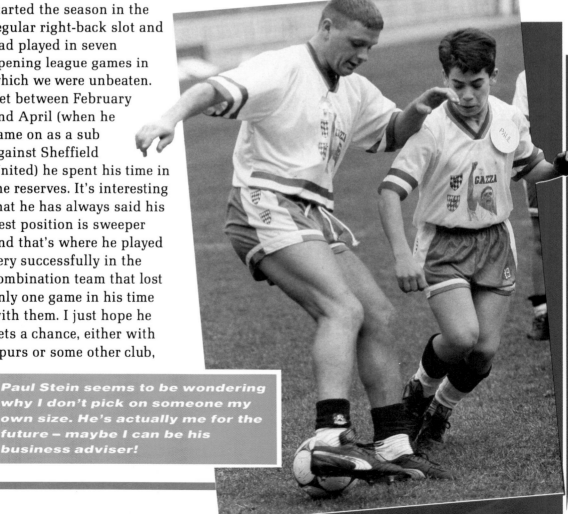

*Paul Stein seems to be wondering why I don't pick on someone my own size. He's actually me for the future – maybe I can be his business adviser!*

to show just how the sweeper system can work when put into action by a classy Continental player.

Chelsea again at the start of March – for the fourth time that season. It's amazing how some teams just haunt you – and yes, you've guessed it, we didn't win. We went a goal down at home again to a Durie effort after twenty minutes, then Gary Lineker equalised just before half time from a penalty. I came off after seventy minutes having been booked yet again. I'm not proud of my disciplinary record but I must say I'm puzzled by it. Contrary to what some people say and think, I do try to keep out of trouble.

Desert Orchid – Dessie – he didn't win the Cup this year, but we did!

Before a match the boss and Gary Mabbutt always have a quiet word, and even Mel and Len, my advisers off the field, who don't usually interfere with football, have a right go at me. It's hard to put into words, but the game and winning mean so much to me that I just have to put every last bit of effort and emotion into everything I think, say or do on the pitch and sometimes that gets misinterpreted (what's that you say, I need an interpreter anyway!) by both officials and fans alike. If I'm upset I'll show it. I did that in Italy and I got made a hero, I've done it in England and been sent off. If I'm happy I'll show it, I did that in Italy and got made a hero. I've done it in England and been told I'm inciting the crowd to riot – you can't win.

On the 11th March I went into hospital and had my operation. I managed to turn the Princess Grace into a madhouse. I'd just got a copy of the video of 'Gazza's Soccer School' and wanted to see it. Everybody at the hospital was great to me and someone put it on. Unfortunately there's only one video channel and one video circuit so everybody who was watching the film of 'The Golden Child' suddenly found it turning into shots of me teaching a load of kids to play football. Some of the more elderly patients are probably still trying to work out the plot to this very day.

It also fitted in quite nicely with Cheltenham week and I had no shortage of visitors wanting to watch the racing on television. At one point, with half a dozen people there (all eating my get-well goodies), and Bryan Robson giving me tips on the phone, it looked more like a betting shop than a hospital room.

There was one particular orderly who brought round the tea. We told him to sit down, poured him a cup of tea and gave him some cake and grapes. He got so relaxed that he forgot why he'd come there in the first place and whether anybody on his rounds got their tea that day I very much doubt.

I got some great get-well presents and cards and if I've not thanked everybody for what they sent me on that particular occasion then I'd like to do so now. It didn't take the pain away but it did make it just that bit easier to bear. Before I had the operation I spoke to Chris Waddle in France.

'Does it hurt Chris?' I asked.
'Nah, not really,' he said, then he paused. 'Well it does hurt a bit when you first come round.'
'Is that it?' I asked, realising that would be bearable.
'Yeah.' A pause. 'But it's a bit painful when they first get you up.'
'Suppose it would be,' I said. 'So there's nothing to it then.'
'Nah. Apart from the pain you get when you first go to the toilet. That's agony.'
'Oh,' I said, wondering if I could escape. Waddle hadn't finished. He was really enjoying himself by now.
'Then they take the stitches out and that's not too funny either. And Gazza, whatever you do, don't laugh.'

I didn't understand what he meant until I spoke to him again after I'd had the operation. He told me some silly joke that wasn't really funny but I started to laugh anyway, felt a pain like a knife turning in my gut, but despite it I couldn't stop laughing. Talk about laughing 'till you cry, I felt I was laughing 'till I died. I just had to put the phone down on him in the end. When Gary Mabbutt was in hospital after the Cup Final also undergoing a hernia operation my first thought in spite of my injury was somehow to get up to him to try and make him laugh but in fact when I spoke to him on the internal telephone he kept hanging up on me!

Eventually they let me go. I got the feeling they weren't going to miss me. The world's press camped outside the hospital and I sent my trusty friend John Coberman out as a decoy in a big car while I sneaked out the back. Call me shy, call me a shrinking violet but there are times when, like Greta Garbo, I just want to be alone! Little did they know that within a matter of months I'd be back again.

# 7

# *French adventures*

I had some time on my hands and after a bit of therapy at the good and effective hands of John Sheridan (the man's a genius) I went off to France to stay with Chris Waddle and his family and to take in the European Cup quarter-final second-leg against AC Milan.

Waddle has a great lifestyle. He lives in a lovely house high up in the hills in a place called Aix-en-Provence and he speaks French so well he can even pronounce the name of the place nowadays! I took my Dad and one of his mates and we had a really good time. The French people were great. I found I could walk around the town or sit in a cafe having a drink without all the hassle I get in England. Even when the Italians

Chris, Lorna and my fiancée, a very young Brooke

turned up for the match it was fine. They all wished me luck in Italy (at least I think that's what they said) and I was quite happy to pose with them for a few souvenir photos.

Lorna, Chris's wife, got a bit fed up with me. We reached a deal over who'd use the phone and when – but I don't think her friends and family appreciated the calls between 2a.m. and 3a.m. which was the only period I left her! There were rumours while I was there that Olympique de Marseille wanted to buy me. Lorna offered to give Spurs whatever Marseille would have paid just to keep me out of the same country as her. Chris and Lorna's little girl Brooke is really lovely. We're engaged to be married so that should put an end to all the rumours about me and other women. Mel and Len brought her a big cuddly toy from England and when they asked her what she was going to call it she didn't hesitate.
'Gazza,' she said.

I didn't see too much of Chris until the night of the match. They take the preparation for games very seriously in France. Lorna says Chris vanishes for weekends with the team (at least that's what he tells her). When Chris first went there he came off the pitch after his first match absolutely shattered. He got dressed and then saw everybody else was still wearing their kit. Papin, their English-speaking international striker, told him that at the end of each game they go back on to the pitch to 'warm down'. Chris thought it was a wind-up and everybody was ganging up on him for a joke, but it wasn't. Back on the pitch he had to go, exhausted though he was.

*Allez Olympique de Marseille. They only won the League, that's all!*

Len, Mel (you can just see his ear behind my left shoulder!) and I arrive at Marseille's stadium for the match against AC Milan

He seems to have settled down very well. All the team like him although they call him 'Roast Beef' and play some dreadful tricks on him – I reckon it's to make him feel at home after all the years he spent rooming with me at Spurs and for England (well somebody has to share a room with me and at least he speaks the same language). When he got recalled to the England team there was a rumour that it was because nobody else would share with me. When Marseille were in Italy to play Milan at the San Siro Stadium Chris got to his room to find his bed upright against the wall and all his clothes standing to attention.

'Did you sleep well Roast Beef?' was the greeting next morning. I can't believe people can play silly tricks like that, can you?

Mel and Len came up for the match and we were driven into Marseille in two cars by a pair of French brothers who owned a local cafe. Mel went in the car in front with an English friend of Chris's and I went in the other brother's car with Len. Now I'm not regarded as the most cautious of drivers, but this guy really thought he was Alain Prost. Somehow or other he kept in touch with his brother ahead and all of a sudden I wished I was back in hospital having my operation all over again – it seemed so much safer. Mel then had the great idea of writing me messages on cards which he held up in the back window of his car. I think our driver must have been a bit short-sighted because he virtually drove bumper to bumper with his brother at 70m.p.h to read such things as 'Gazza you're a waste of money' or 'We all believe Brock is better than Gazza'. He's Newcastle daft that bloke.

Anyway we got to the ground and arrived just in time to see Chris and the rest of the team coming off the coach.

'Behave yourself Gazza,' was all he said to me, 'I have to live here.'

The game was great and Chris was brilliant. I sat in the VIP box with Graham Taylor and Lawrie McMenemy who'd come to watch Chris. We don't really hear enough of his popularity back in England. Over in France he's a folk hero. They call him 'Le Magicien' and every time his name is mentioned he gets an enormous cheer. Whenever he gets the ball a buzz goes round the ground, very much like it used to in his last season at Spurs. Everybody said Olympique de Marseille were crazy to pay £4.5 million for him, but believe me he's proved he's worth every penny and more.

I was very impressed by everything I saw and heard at the stadium that night. The catering in our box was terrific and I didn't think I was going to find room for the celebration meal that was to follow. As it worked out it was lucky I did have something to eat beforehand. Chris scored a great goal then got a terrible knock with a

Chris Waddle, flagging a bit

**Guillit calls it a day for AC Milan against Marseille**

rabbit-punch to the back of the head. He went down as if he'd been hit by Frank Bruno and when they brought him round he promptly got fouled again and went down once more. He then headed the ball and looked in trouble, but went on the most brilliant run that could well have ended with the goal of the season if he hadn't been fouled. The lights then failed, Milan stormed off claiming they couldn't see when Stevie Wonder could probably have played out the last few minutes, and as everybody knows they found themselves with a European ban.

The crowd went mad and I honestly thought the whole stadium was about to explode. What was really nice was seeing so many Union Jacks amongst the Olympique de Marseille banners actually being carried by Frenchmen as a tribute to Chris.

We all trooped off to the reception afterwards and I was flattered to see the label on the bottle of wine read 'Vin de Pays des Côtes de Gascogne'. Nice of them to bother.

Len spent most of the evening peeling them off and getting me to sign them. They'd imported a famous French chef who'd concocted a meal of twelve courses. They had minders on the doors to keep out the press, including one guy who was an ex-boxer and who had fought our Alan Minter for a world title. He showed me the size of his hands and they made Peter Shilton's look like a toddler's. The English Press boys aren't easily put off and one or two of them did actually get in (special award to Rob Shepherd of *Today* who even got to the bar.)

As each player came in there was an enormous cheer but the biggest of all was reserved for Chris. I don't think he even heard it. He looked terrible, absolutely white, and he's not got much colour at the best of times. In fact I've seen healthier looking ghosts.

'I'm all right,' he said, 'I've just got a bit of a headache.' He suddenly slumped forward and buried his head in his arms.

'Bloody typical,' I said, 'you invite all these people out to dinner and you can't even be bothered to talk to us.'

By now we'd been joined by Glenn Hoddle and whether it was the thought of having to sing 'Diamond Lights' or whether it was my company I don't know, but Chris suddenly felt the need for fresh air. Papin led him outside and I didn't think it was fair to leave him without some English company so I followed him. They know how to treat their invalids in France. There on the steps to the restaurant someone had put a bed.

'Get up on the bed, Waddler,' I said, 'pose for a few photos, it'll be a laugh.'

Chris wasn't seeing the funny side by now. He'd actually gone a couple of extra shades of white if that is possible and even Lorna was beginning to look a bit worried. The club doctor called for an ambulance.

'Don't let Gazza come with me to the hospital,' was all Chris was saying. It's funny the effect a knock on the head can have on you! He seemed almost happy to be led off into the ambulance and afterwards I heard somebody saying he'd only gone to hospital to get away from me.

I went back to the party but the magic had gone out of the night despite the presence of a top-rate magician who went from table to table. His best trick of the night I suppose was making Chris disappear. We'd only got through four courses by midnight and I was feeling really tired after my operation, so Mel, Len, Glenn and I all left. As it happened Olympique de Marseille didn't make an offer for me and that was the end of my little French adventure. Lorna Waddle, you can breathe again!

# 8

# The season winds down

After the sixth-round Cup match the Spurs team were just marking time in the league. I don't mean they weren't trying; even if it's only a friendly, a professional footballer is conditioned to go out there and do his best – that's a matter of pride – it was just a case of looking to the Cup for the best chance of success. We'd lost 3–2 at Villa, a vital win for Graham Taylor's old club which, looking back, probably kept them in the First Division. We drew 0–0 at home to Queen's Park Rangers, not a bad result as Rangers were in the middle of their purple patch of form, and then drew 2–2 at home to Coventry with Nayim scoring both goals. I'm always surprised Nayim doesn't get more goals – when he goes forward he always looks dangerous. He's come on a bundle and has added a bit of English guts to his Continental skills. It's hard to think now that I was given the job of teaching him English when he first came over. For the first three months in the country he couldn't understand why everyone was shocked when he tried

Nayim makes the ball talk – but does it speak Spanish?

to speak to them in English. Now he knows that I only taught him swear words and he speaks English better than I do (not difficult, I hear you say?).

I was pleased that Phil Gray, the young Irishman, got a chance in my absence. He's been very unlucky with his injuries since he's been at the club and I think in time he'll turn out to be a very good player. Having started games against Queen's Park Rangers and Coventry, he was back as substitute against Luton where David Tuttle made his second appearance of the season. It's really good to see kids coming through rather than big name signings. There was a time when I was at Newcastle when nearly all the team were local lads. It was only when players came from 'abroad', that is anywhere south of Hartlepool, that the crowd started to distance themselves from the team. David Howells was the only trainee sourced player to start the first match of the season for Spurs but gradually, as the season developed, the names of players like Ian Hendon, John Moncur, Ian Walker, Tuttle and Gray began to appear. If Tottenham's cash problems did nothing else, at least they began to give the kids a chance. Ian Walker, the goalie, is a real prospect and has already attracted international attention at Under-21 level, even though he only played once this season; but he's nine years younger than Erik the Viking and his time will come.

Arsenal are a prime example of how to blend youngsters with experienced purchases. Tony Adams, Michael Thomas, Paul Davis, David Hillier, David Rocastle, Kevin Campbell, Paul Merson, David O'Leary – not one of them cost a penny and all played for the club at junior level. Put them with the likes of David Seaman, Steve Bould, Nigel Winterburn, Anders Limpar and Alan Smith and you've got a Championship-winning side.

While others were doing business on the field I was doing my best to get fit to get back on to it. Without me, the team finally got back to winning ways against Southampton on the 6th April which was, incredibly, our first home league win of the year. You had to go back to the 22nd December against Luton to find us last picking up three points at White Hart Lane. Four days after the Southampton victory, on the 10th April, just four weeks after I'd had my operation, I started the match against Norwich. But we weren't absolutely at full strength just a week before the semis; there were only five survivors of the team who had started the season so confidently and optimistically in the August sunshine against Manchester City.

Power put Norwich ahead before a young Scottish signing, John Hendry, equalised on his debut. I came off after sixty-two minutes, feeling tired but happy to be back. Peter Garland, another youth product, made his debut to replace me and although the team played well, Norwich's experience showed through to give them a 2–1 victory with a goal by Spurs old boy Ian Crook nine minutes from time.

After the famous semi-final I did have a slight reaction in my groin and I only played

55 minutes against Palace, this time coming off for John Hendry. We lost 1–0 and Palace were close to making sure of third place in the league. They had a great season when you consider Liverpool beat them 9–0 in September 1989, while last season they finished just a few points and one place behind them in the league. Nigel Martyn must play for England one day, Geoff Thomas and Ian Wright already do, and John Salako has impressed on the summer tour. Andy Thorn has added a bit of steel at the back – as if any were really necessary when they've got Eric Young! The thing about Palace is that, although they have a reputation for being a bit physical (and they did show that side of their nature in the 1990 Cup Final replay and last season's Zenith Data Final), they do also have some players who can play good football.

Ian Wright looking for his first full England cap

I missed the games against Sheffield United and Everton as it was felt I still needed more time to get back to fitness. Sheffield United played much better than they'd done back in October and drew 2–2 and it was nice to see Justin Edinburgh score his first goal for the club. The 3–3 draw with Everton was a cracker and I was sorry I missed it. I was also sorry that more attention was paid to why I wasn't playing, whether I'd be going, whether I'd be staying, than to the game itself. If you read some of the press reports from the following day it was almost as if the match hadn't happened and the 21,675 fans had just turned up to see me sitting in the stands.

We had our Cup Final rehearsal on the 4th May and although the papers said Forest slaughtered us it didn't feel that way on the pitch. We drew 1–1 and everybody felt the best was yet to come at Wembley.

When we'd first looked down the fixture list, we'd hoped our last match against Liverpool would be the Championship decider. It wasn't to be. Arsenal had the title safely under their belts and we weren't even in contention for a place in the UEFA Cup. Although it's nice – and good for football – that Liverpool are back in Europe, you have to feel sorry for Palace. They started the season thinking that as long as Liverpool were to be second they only had to come third to qualify. Then UEFA let Liverpool back in and of course, most unfair of all, English clubs only get one automatic qualifier in the UEFA Cup. Although I might be a bit biased in favour of Italian football at the moment I can still see it's crazy that the Italians, with a smaller league and a worse track record, have seven clubs in the UEFA Cup and we have one.

*I'd like to say what it feels like to celebrate a Cup Final victory, but I can't*

Liverpool won 2–0 although it was actually a bit closer than that. We got through without serious injury and the only match left was against Manchester United.

In fact, of course, I took no part in that game but both teams treated it as a celebration. United had just won the Cup Winners' Cup and we had the trophy that had taken them into that competition in the first place. The game quite properly finished 1–1 and Tottenham were able to look forward to the next season in Europe with a chance of actually meeting Manchester

United in the competition. All credit to Alex Ferguson – there had to be a moment last season when he was a game or two away from the chop and there he is having guided United into the top six in the First Division, to a Rumbelows Cup Final and a European triumph. Lee Sharpe is obviously an exciting young prospect, but in Steve Bruce and Gary Pallister he's developed two defenders to a real level of maturity. And spare a thought for Les Sealey; he's come from Luton reserves to win a Cup winner's medal, a European medal, a Rumbelows Cup runners-up medal, all in twelve months – not bad for someone whose career seemed to be going nowhere. Les is one of football's unsung heroes and I'm really pleased it's come right for him so late in his career. Mark Hughes had a magnificent season capped with a great goal in the Cup Winner's Cup Final. He fully deserved his Footballer of the Year Award. So there it was, another league season ended, although with the play-offs the final pieces of the jigsaw had yet to be put into place. Come August it all starts again, everybody equal. I'm just sorry that I won't be there kicking a ball on that first Saturday of the season.

# Early Cup moments

The Cup starts a long time before the likes of Spurs get involved, but of all the little teams that started their Cup runs around the time we were kicking off our league programme against Manchester City, only three got through to the third round: Barrow, Woking and my special favourites, Barnet.

Barrow of the GM Vauxhall Conference put up a brave fight before going down 1–0 to Bolton, and given Bolton's high final position in the Third Division, that was no mean feat. Kenny Lowe, who played for them that day transferred to Barnet later in the season and is now a league player. I thought in any event he could well follow the list of ex-Barnet players who have made it into the league successfully: such footballers as Robert Codner, Andrew Clarke, David Regis, Paul Harding, Phil Gridelet and Lee Payne (who went to Newcastle before joining Reading).

Barnet were actually outclassed 5–0 on the day by Portsmouth on their difficult slope at Underhill. However, in a way that was a blessing in disguise because it enabled them to concentrate on the league. When they were fifteen points behind Kettering at Christmas everybody wrote them off, then when Kettering blew up and Altrincham and Colchester pushed Barnet down to third place it looked again as if they were going to be the bridesmaid and never the bride. Then suddenly things fell right for them; Altrincham, having gone twenty-seven games without defeat, suddenly lost two and drew one including a vital game at Slough when after being 3–1 up they let in an 89th minute equaliser. Colchester and Kettering killed each other off and Barnet won six of the last seven matches.

It was a great season for North London; Spurs at Wembley (twice!), Arsenal Champions and Barnet in the league. Barnet had their own 'Cup Final' against Fisher on the last Saturday of the season. There are loads of Spurs and Arsenal supporters who also support Barnet and the lads and I took a real interest in that match. Fisher were relegated already and had nothing to lose. Barnet had beaten them 8–1 in the home match and it must have seemed like the perfect fixture as far as they were concerned. Some hopes! They went 1–0 down, then equalised, then went 2–1 down. Meanwhile Colchester, the only team who could catch them, were 2–0 up. Then Barnet's Dave Howell, a non-league veteran, got the equaliser and finally Gary Bull, Steve's cousin, got two to bring his tally for the season to thirty. It'll be interesting to see what Bull and Barnet do in the league next year. They actually played Arsenal's first team in a celebration friendly at the end of the season and until they started

messing around with substitutes they gave as good as they got. One thing sure is that Stan Flashman will bring a bit of colour to directors' boxes up and down the country – always assuming he can get a ticket to allow him in! Mind you with Stan's figure it's a bit necessary to have 'three together' – sorry Stanley!

If Barrow and Barnet were disappointed in the Cup, the same wasn't true of Woking. I remember they've had a few Cup runs, including a saga against Barnet a few years ago during the course of which one Jimmy Greaves (late of Tottenham now of Saint and ...) was sent off for throwing a perfect right hook. I've always said that young Greavsie had a suspect temperament – I can't really say anything nasty about Jimmy because he's such a nice bloke and has always been one of my biggest supporters. This time they took on West Bromwich Albion and walloped them 4–2 at the Hawthorns. It meant the end for Albion's player-manager Brian Talbot, and it wasn't exactly their year because, although Bobby Gould took over he couldn't stop them sliding down into the Third Division for the first time in their history. A shame that, because every West Bromwich side I've ever seen has tried to play football and the Third Division is much easier to get into than to get out of. A young man called Tim Buzaglo scored a hat-trick that'll be shown on telly as often as the Hereford goal that put Newcastle out of the Cup in the 1970s. Inevitably the papers immediately nicknamed him 'Buzza'. Tim was an unusual hero to say the least. He's actually played international cricket – for Gibraltar – and worked as a computer operator by day. He nearly programmed the defeat of Everton in the fourth round but the giant killers went out 1–0 at Goodison, yet did nothing but good for themselves and non-league football. Long may the Wokings of this world succeed in the Cup – as long as it's not against any team I play for!

Meanwhile Spurs' progress in the Cup was a bit less dramatic. When you look back from the Final you always remember the odd heart-stopping moment when it looked as if it was going to be all over. Our third-round game was away to Blackpool where Paul Stewart had started his career – he actually played over 200 league games there before he moved on to Manchester City. In January the focus was more on Tottenham's problems off the pitch but, as I've said in the league review of the year, we hadn't been doing too well on it. We'd lost all of our last three games and in fact lost five out of the last seven. I'd covered myself in glory with a televised sending off and every journalist

**Buzza's Bonanza! Tim Buzaglo gets three for Woking against West Bromwich Albion in the Cup**

in the country was licking his lips just waiting for Blackpool to put us out.

Whenever you think of Blackpool it's either rock or Sir Stanley Matthews that comes to mind. I'd have loved to have played on the same side as Stan. I've seen film of him, in particular a 4–3 Cup Final in 1953 when it looked as if he had the ball tied to his feet. Blackpool in January is more like Antarctica; a muddy pitch, howling winds, freezing rain, just the sort of weather for a bit of giant killing. Only this time we got away with it. Although we only won 1–0, with a goal from Stewey against his old club, it was enough, and although they had a few chances so did we and nobody came away saying we were lucky. Paul Groves in midfield for Blackpool caught my eye. I suppose I tend to see more of the midfield opposition than the rest of the team but I thought he did very well.

You always wait for the draw for the next round with bated breath. Would it be Liverpool, would it be Woking? It was Oxford actually, and although it was at home I, at least, didn't expect them to be a

*The Wembley genius himself*

*Flying high against Oxford in the Cup*

pushover. I'd seen them play the previous season at home to Newcastle when they'd won and I rated both John Durnin and Paul Simpson. Stewey knew all about Simpson because he'd played alongside him at Manchester City. As it happened, their Man of the Match against us was neither of them but Les Phillips who I thought had a terrific game. Gary Mabbutt put us ahead with one of his rare but typical efforts, then Gary Lineker made it 2–0. You fancy yourself to win comfortably when you're 2–0 up at home after twenty minutes against a team from a lower division but Oxford never gave up. Martin Foyle pulled one back before half time, I made it 3–1 and then Foyle got another. It wasn't until I scored a second four minutes from the end that we finally saw them off, and even then not before they'd given us a fright or two. It really didn't surprise me that they did so well in the second half of the season in Division Two and I reckon they'll be pushing for promotion this year.

The fifth round had us away again. This time to the conquerors of Barnet – Portsmouth. Like Blackpool, they're a great club who've fallen on slightly hard times – although perhaps not quite as hard. They've had their spell in the Third Division but they'd finished mid-table in the Second the previous season and didn't look as if they were either relegation or promotion candidates this time round. They do have incredible support down on the south coast and 'The Pompey Chimes' sung properly is probably the next best thing to 'The Blaydon Races'. Spurs had played them five years before in the Milk Cup and had their problems and this time our problems started before the whistle even blew for the kick-off. Terry Fenwick fell over heavily while we were warming up and broke his ankle – yet another blow to his injury-strewn career. We quickly regrouped and then fell behind just before half time to a goal by Mark Chamberlain.

Mark's an interesting character. He started off at Port Vale, then went on to Stoke. Whilst there he played for England eight times. In fact for quite a while he was preferred to Chris Waddle before he seemed to lose form after an injury in 1985. He ended up at Portsmouth via Sheffield Wednesday and at half time, with us 1–0 down and quite frankly playing poorly, his form didn't look too bad to me.

*Glory, glory Tottenham Hotspur*

The Pompey roar was getting louder all the time from the 26,000 crowd – the biggest since they'd last played Spurs. Before this match it wasn't so much a question of whether or not we'd be the victors or victims of giant killers, but rather whether or not Spurs would survive financially if we went out of the Cup. Now I think I speak for all the players when I say that when we get out there on a Saturday afternoon what goes on in the boardroom or the bank is of no concern to us – but what none of us was prepared to do was to let our pride be damaged and be known as the players who let down Spurs and their supporters. I've said throughout my own on-off transfer saga that no player is bigger than the club and no team is bigger than the club either. In twenty years time there'll be another bunch of lads wearing Spurs shirts but the true Tottenham supporter will still be watching them week-in, week-out even if he has to sit rather than stand on his favourite terraces.

We came out for that second half to play for our pride and the pride of Tottenham and I was really pleased with both my goals, one scored on the hour and another six minutes from the end; I was even more flattered when BBC's Match of the Day put them to music – not even my songs either. Guy Whittingham, who'd virtually destroyed Barnet on his own, had one of the disappointing matches that every striker

*Our Mitch gets the better of Dean Yates of Notts County in the Cup. This season they can have a rematch in the league*

suffers from time to time, but still I think in due course one of the bigger clubs will pick him up and he'll be a better and sharper player at a higher level. Graeme Hogg impressed me the most here, playing at the back sometimes, then moving up into midfield. He started at Manchester United, and in fact had seemed to be a regular there before the importation of some expensive signings, and at twenty-seven I think he's just beginning to reach his peak.

I don't like the way the Cup draw's done at the moment. Nothing can beat the old Monday lunchtime tradition. I remember when I was at school, everybody used to smuggle their trannies in and write the draw out as soon as it was made, then try and be the first out into the playground to broadcast the news. Now we've all sold out to TV again, and not even to a station that everybody can receive. What with that, and what with a round being spread over two, three or sometimes four days it's all a bit messy. Let's get back to the old basics I say – all the matches on a Saturday (maybe one in the evening if it has to be televised live) and the draw on the radio on Monday, giving all the players all day Sunday to dream about what might be.

What there was for us in the sixth round was Notts County, the game to be played – yes you've guessed it – for the benefit of television on Sunday the 10th March. I knew, even before the game, that win or lose I'd have to go into hospital to have my hernia operation. We'd worked out that if we won we had exactly five weeks until the semi-final for me to get fit again – just about enough time if I worked at it really hard. But when O'Riordan put County ahead five minutes before half time all that looked academic. I was playing up front by then because I simply couldn't cover the normal amount of ground. Terry lifted us at half time not by giving us a rollicking but just by telling us to keep at it. After fifty-one minutes Nayim brought us level and then, summoning up my last drains of energy, I scored the winner. We were through. For County, Mark Draper was terrific, skilful on the ball and a good distributor; he's only 19 and I'm sure will go far in the game. County of course had a wonderful season, winning the play-off final to gain promotion to the First Division, and with the steel that Paul Harding gives them at the back I'm sure they'll do well this season. A lot was made of my tangle with Paul. He gave me a hard game and I gave him a hard knock and yet we're still talking to each other and, as you'll see elsewhere in this book, he was one of those kind enough to talk about me. Dave Regis didn't play against us because he was cup-tied, having appeared for Barnet, but Paul and Dave, as Barnet old boys, show how easy it is nowadays for Conference players to slot into the league. Andy Hunt from Kettering ended the season as a fixture in the Newcastle side, Ian Woan from Runcorn played for Forest in the Cup Final, and when Brighton played County in the Second Division play-off final they had Robert Codner and Nicky Bissett, also ex-Barnet players.

Anyway, there we were through to the semi-final and there I was in the Princess Grace Hospital.

# 10
## *Semi-final glory*

As I lay in the Princess Grace in March I had no idea that it wasn't to be my final visit of the year. They say everything comes in threes. I reckon I really had three lots of treatment at the hospital. First of all there was my injection treatment – that didn't work – then the hernia operation and finally the knee. Enough's enough. Having seen a video of my knee operation I'm thinking of putting it on sale for £9.99 and calling it 'Gazza's Gory'.

I always believed in my heart of hearts that I'd be fit for the semis although obviously, as far as the media are concerned, you have to be a bit careful. Give them a line and they make a whole front page out of it. I was particularly keen to play when I knew it was to be Arsenal that we'd face and when the FA quite rightly made Wembley the venue it guaranteed all of the players at least one Wembley Cup appearance in the season.

The other semi was to be between Forest and West Ham. The Hammers had seen off Everton 2–1 with what I'm told was an excellent performance and showed just what a loss they are to the First Division. *Shoot!* magazine gave Stuart Slater ten out of ten for his performance and it's hardly surprising that a few foreign clubs are showing an interest in him. However, I always felt that a promotion chase and a Cup run would be too much to keep up and I was right, although being reduced to ten men in the semi-final didn't really help West Ham's cause.

As our own semi approached, I gradually got myself back to fitness and by the time of the match I reckon I was about 70 per cent there. Normally you don't play when you're not 100 per cent fit, but in this case the Boss decided to take a chance on me and it paid off in spades. We were all really fired up for the semi. You don't need a lot of talking to in order to want to beat Arsenal. In a way, drawing them was the best thing that could have happened to us because it was North London's final and it was being played at Wembley.

I think, looking back, we treated it more seriously than Arsenal. Everybody said they were going to win, they were beginning to look certainties for the league and when they turned up wearing lounge suits it was as if they'd already done the job and were in the Final. We wore our tracksuits, and although it later proved not to be the case, we were really mad when we heard they'd already recorded their Cup Final song. The atmosphere at Wembley was fantastic, in fact better than on the day of the actual

Final. The ground was filled with supporters of both teams who'd come to watch a game of football, rather than come for a social day out.

We really rose to it and slaughtered Arsenal for half an hour. After five minutes we got a free kick. I never thought for a moment of doing anything else but having a strike at goal. I know a lot of people have told me they thought I couldn't score against the England keeper from there but I reckoned I could and I did. In fact when I spoke to Dave Seaman on the phone from the hospital after the Final I had the cheek to ask him why he'd made himself look silly by going for the ball! It wasn't the first goal I'd scored from that position at Wembley. Whilst I'd been filming my *Soccer School* video with the kids I'd taken a whole series of free kicks just from that position against young Andrew Quy and Paul Sheridan (John's son). Now while neither of them would claim to be David Seaman the principle's the same and it worked. Who says my commercial activities interfere with my football?

*Take that! My free kick against Arsenal in the semi-final*

Me, with all my pop experience, leading Gary Mabbutt, Mitchell Thomas and Steve Sedgley

The second goal gave me a fair amount of pleasure as well. A 1–2 with Paul Allen, then Gary Lineker putting in a typical effort. Two-nil up and only ten minutes gone. We were a bit disappointed when Smithy got one back for the Gunners just before half time but Terry warned us of the pressure we'd be under in the second half and he wasn't wrong. They came at us, but our defence, and Gary Mabbutt in particular, were magnificent and we broke away fifteen minutes from the end for Gary Lineker to score his second, the third for the team. By then I was off, having done my job. I can't ever remember watching a match so intently after being substituted. Normally I can't stand being taken off and I also can't stand being a spectator; but this was a different class, this was something else. At the end I remember running on to the pitch and cuddling Terry Venables and Dougie Livermore, then lifting Stewey up as if he were the FA Cup itself – mind you with his weight I could have done my hernia in all over again. I made sure I shook hands with all the Arsenal players and gave them a consoling pat. I know exactly how they felt and although there's great rivalry between the clubs the players get on very well.

I gave a short and sweet interview to television just telling them how I'd been unable to sleep the night before and then saying I had to dash off to get my new suit

measured for the Final. I just wanted to be with the Boss and the lads, I was so happy and excited. Looking back at the season, that really was the best moment and in a way it was almost all downhill from then on. We went off to celebrate, my Mum, my Dad and I, although it was tinged with sadness because during the week my Grandad Fred had died after a long illness. It had been awful for my Dad just waiting for the worst and I felt that somehow I'd helped to ease his pain.

The build-up to the Final started almost immediately. People criticised the whole idea of a 'team pool' but quite frankly if you've worked hard to achieve something as we had I can't see anything wrong with trying to make a bit of money out of it. We had a real laugh making the record with Chas and Dave and although it didn't get as high as 'Fog on the Tyne' or 'Geordie Boys' it did mean I'd 'sung'(?!) on four records in one year that had got into the Top 100 (you'd forgotten the World Cup song, hadn't you?). Now I reckon that has to be some kind of record(?!) for a professional footballer.

In the evening of the recording we went to watch Gary Stretch fight Chris Eubank. I'm a great Eubank fan myself so I was a bit embarrassed when my invitation came from Clare Tomlinson at Gary's PR company Max Clifford Associates – but we still had a good time and the Spurs players who were there, Mitchell Thomas, Steve Sedgley, David Howells, Gary Lineker and Paul Stewart, were left in no doubt by the crowd as to how many friends we'd won by getting to the Final.

Everybody had been saying how the things that were happening off the field would affect us. They never did in a negative way, it just made us all the more determined to win something for our club and to keep the club going for its supporters.

Although at the time the days seemed to drag by, leading up to the Final, looking back now it all went too quickly. The transfer speculation never stopped but somehow or other I managed to keep it out of my mind. I always worked on the basis that as soon as the Final was over, one way or another I'd make up mind. I even told Mel and Len not to tell me the proposed terms from Lazio because I wanted to keep concentrating on the Final.

# Cup of triumph and tears

Everybody dreams of playing in a Wembley Final and, yes, I was hyped-up for the match. Apart from the fact there was a chance it was going to be my last match with Spurs, I desperately wanted to help win the Cup for my team-mates, the supporters and perhaps most of all Terry Venables and his team – Dougie Livermore, John Sheridan, Dave Butler, Ted Buxton, Ray Clemence and so many more. I'd given about 120 tickets to friends and family, my whole allocation and some more I'd scrounged from other members of the squad. Don't believe the stories you hear of players making vast profits from Cup Final tickets. I don't know one of my team-mates who sold a ticket at a profit, and in fact most of them actually paid for some tickets and then gave them away.

When you're a kid you think about playing in a Cup Final – but you know it's not

The Spurs front bench – but I can't bear to look

possible. When you're a pro you know you can do it and I was about to fulfil that dream. I'd always said before that the World Cup semi-final was the biggest day of my life, but with the FA Cup Final being in your own country everybody looks forward to it – not just the fans of the teams taking part, but millions of fans all over the country who are going to get the beers in and sit in front of their televisions.

Before the game it was billed as 'The Gazza-Clough Final'. At the end of the day it belonged to neither of us – one was a loser and the other was in hospital. Yet for both of us it was a first time in a Cup Final, and at least I got a winner's medal. I've enormous respect for Brian Clough, he's won just about everything there is to win in the game – but at least he's still got that elusive Cup win to look forward to. Without that, perhaps he might have retired by now which would be the game's loss.

Forest had a terrific run up to the Final, scoring hatfuls of goals in the league and stringing together a long unbeaten sequence. Everybody was fighting for their place in the team and it's incredible to think that Roy Keane, who'd done so much to get them to Wembley, only just scraped into the team ahead of Steve Hodge. Poor old Steve found himself in the England squad whilst only on the bench for Forest! But then it's typical of Cloughie, he's not one for reputations and he's not scared to do what he thinks is right. I do think, however, that if he'd shown a bit more emotion from the bench the Forest kids might have reacted differently. All the managers I've played under expend more energy from the touchline than most of their players do on the field – Arthur Cox in particular – but Cloughie just sits there impassively and if any of his team are struggling and look towards him for guidance they're not going to get it. He obviously thinks that he's done all his work before the match and should leave his team to get on with it on the day. It's one approach and it must work, because otherwise he wouldn't be as successful as he is – but it didn't work in the Final.

Before the game I was introduced to Princess Di. I asked if I could kiss her hand, she blushed a bit. I asked again and she said yes, so I did; and then I couldn't leave out the Duchess of Kent, could I? So I

*Clough – leader of the Green Party*

kissed her hand as well. It was all a far cry from a day in November when I attended a charity lunch, and got very upset when I was told that the Palace didn't want the Princess and I in the same room in case I cuddled her like I cuddled Maggie Thatcher. I found that quite insulting because I wouldn't be so stupid as to do something like that without asking permission first. I'm sure that had nothing to do with the Princess – if she goes to a charity do then, like me, all she's interested in is raising money for the charity, not who is or isn't there or what stories the Press might make of it. I feel really sorry for her because her life's not her own thanks to the Press.

When the whistle's finally blown to start a Final it's just another match, ninety minutes of football against a team which, in this case, we'd already played twice that season. They were only human, only footballers like us trying to do their best to win the game. The first moment of controversy as far as I was concerned was the Garry Parker tackle. I went for the ball, played the ball, and couldn't help but follow it through. I never set out to top anybody; I know how bad it is for any player to be injured especially in a Final. I've watched the replay and it does look much worse than

it was; but nobody would have said very much about it if it had been anybody apart from me or Vinnie Jones. In fact I asked Roger Milford, the referee, why he'd given a free kick when I'd won the ball but he just smiled.

The Gary Charles incident was only a few minutes later. I thought he was going to take the ball on, and I ran too far and totally mis-timed the tackle when he was too quick for me. Our instructions were to get stuck in, to be first, to win every tackle. I was determined to follow them to the letter and all I was trying to do was win the ball. I didn't even think of what might or might not happen to him or me. The really aggravating thing was that Pat van den Hauwe had the move covered and would have won the ball, which made my involvement totally unnecessary.

My knee didn't hurt at first. I felt more worried for Charles than myself because I thought I might have damaged his shin. A young lad like him playing in his first Final – it would have been a tragedy, but up he got and up I got. I took my place in the wall, Stuart Pearce blasted the ball and the ref didn't notice the foul that took Gary

*Above: The worst moment of my life*
*Left: Gary Mabbutt taken out and a gap appears in the wall*

Mabbutt out of the line and let the ball through. Although I felt guilty at giving away the free-kick I didn't really have a lot of time to think about it because suddenly I felt that my knee was loose. I asked Steve Sedgley to pass me the ball, he did and I went down and really started worrying. It was the most frightening experience of my life. I kept hoping that I'd just jarred it but in my heart of hearts I knew it was serious.

John Sheridan came over and checked it out and I kept saying to him: 'Am I going to be alright?' I could see in his face that he didn't want to tell me the truth.

I was taken to the special hospital room at the stadium and all I could think about was that the Wembley hoodoo had struck again. All players are superstitious and in fact somebody I knew just a week or two before had touched me with his crutch. That, in my book, is bad luck and it's incredible over the last forty years how many times a player has been seriously injured in a Cup Final. Wally Barnes of Arsenal did his knee ligaments in 1952, Eric Bell of Bolton in 1953, Billy Meadows was badly hurt playing for Manchester City in 1955 against Newcastle, Bert Trautmann, again for City, broke his neck in 1956, Ray Wood of Manchester United fractured his jaw in 1957, Harry

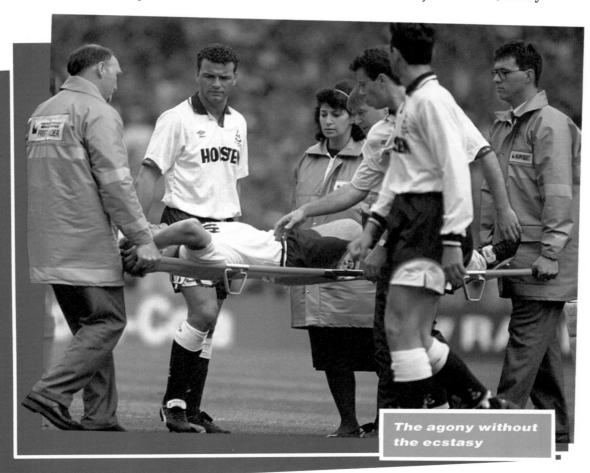

The agony without the ecstasy

Gregg, also of United, was injured in 1958 and Roy Dwight broke a leg in 1959. Dave Whelan of Blackburn broke a leg in 1960 and Len Chalmers' injury in 1961 meant Spurs beat a 10-man Leicester. For all the years since then the jinx seemed to have died, but jinxes never die they just take a rest. It was my turn in 1991. I just hope I've not started things off all over again.

I think that might just be a foul, ref

Down in the room I heard two roars and I thought the worst. I wasn't to know that one was for Gary Lineker's 'offside' goal that TV showed was perfectly good, and the other for his penalty miss. I kept thinking about the lads up on the pitch, willing them to win, praying we weren't 3–0 down. Glen Roeder brought my mother down to me and she was in a terrible state. I really didn't want her to see me as I was and I sent her back up, telling her I'd rather she was supporting the lads than watching me.

John Browett, the surgeon, came to look at me and told me he'd have to operate. All I can remember saying is 'That's life, that's football,' but I think I was in some state of shock. I was in agony but I begged to be allowed back up to watch the game from a wheelchair. It should have been the best day of my life but I'd only seen fifteen minutes of it. They weren't having any of it as they thought I might do myself a greater injury (I'm not sure how much worse I could have made it!). I found myself in an ambulance on my way to the Princess Grace hospital in the West End. I kept asking the ambulance driver the score and he told me we'd equalised but he didn't know who'd scored. As soon as I got to hospital I wanted the TV on and I had to keep telling the nurse who was trying to make me comfortable to get out of the way so I could watch the match.

I was amazed at how on top we were. Paul Stewart was unbelievable (he must surely play for England soon) and although it's not fair to mention individual players I have to add Paul Allen and Gary Mabbutt to my list of Wembley greats – but at the end of the day it was a team effort.

Right inset: Paul Stewart caps his man of the match performance with a goal
Below: You can beat our Des Walker

I got a bottle of champagne and shared it with Mr Gilmour who'd done my hernia operation. I had tears in my eyes but I'd not cried. The press, of course, said I did, but I had my face covered on the stretcher, so how could they know? I was in shock, miles away, just thinking 'What am I doing on a stretcher?' People were talking to me but I wasn't listening.

Later in hospital, the match won, I phoned Peter Barnes the Club Secretary, on his mobile and spoke to Stewey in the dressing room. I told him to tell the lads to enjoy themselves, to have a good night, forget about me, but to look after my family.

'Don't worry,' Stewey said, 'I'll have your Mum dancing' – and he did.

The whole team stopped at the hospital and gave me my medal. They let me hold the cup and as I kissed it I saw a few of the lads with tears in their eyes. Although I was delighted they'd come I was also quite pleased when they'd gone because I felt I was spoiling their day. I just wanted them to get on with enjoying themselves and I wanted to be alone. It was when they left I started to cry and for three hours I couldn't stop, and although I begged and pleaded to be allowed to go to the celebrations for just five minutes, it wasn't to be. They had to get Mr Browett back to convince me it would be

**Who says Spurs are a one-man team?**

dangerous. I did manage to call Chris Waddle, John Sheridan and Marilyn Stein (poor Mel was walking back from Wembley without any means of knowing what was going on) and they all got floods of emotion down the telephone.

Although I couldn't go on the team's victory tour it was great to know I wasn't forgotten. The phone didn't stop ringing. Ray Wilkins called and said 'You'll get over it. The way you came out of the double hernia this'll be a doddle.' Then Peter Beardsley called and so did Steve McMahon, Mark Wright, Paul Parker – all the England team in fact, plus the likes of Arthur Cox who still regards me as one of his 'babes'. Eventually the hospital had to cut off calls and visitors, though by the end of the week every member of the Spurs squad had visited me. That in itself made me feel so much better. It's at times like these that you realise just who your true friends are.

It's the same with the Press. Some of them took extra pleasure in having a go at me knowing I couldn't hit back. They know who I mean. While some writers took the time and trouble to send me good wishes and to write sensible sympathetic articles. I'd particularly like to thank Rob Shepherd of *Today*, Charlie Sale at the *Express*, John Richardson of the *Sun* and, surprisingly enough, Harry Harris of the *Mirror*, with whom I've not always seen eye to eye. Curiously enough it was the so-called quality

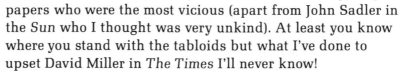

papers who were the most vicious (apart from John Sadler in the *Sun* who I thought was very unkind). At least you know where you stand with the tabloids but what I've done to upset David Miller in *The Times* I'll never know!

I spent the next week concentrating on getting my knee better, doing exactly what Mr Browett ordered (even to the point of no alcohol). I knew it wasn't weeks but months that I'd have to work on it. I made up my mind I'd be patient. I'd be a perfect patient and I'd be back. It was Bryan Robson who gave me the greatest comfort of all. Nobody could have been written off as often as he's been, yet he's struggled back from each injury better than ever, not just to represent Manchester United but also to regain the England captaincy. He said, 'Gazza, you'll be not just a better player, you'll be a better person.'

I know I'm not Pelé, but I'm not George Best either. I'm me, Paul Gascoigne, and that's who I want to be when I get back to playing again; but a Paul Gascoigne who's had time to think things over, to work out his future for himself. One thing's for certain, my future won't hold another tackle like that one on the 18th May 1991.

# 12
## The International year

On the 12th September England played a friendly against Hungary, the first under new manager Graham Taylor. It seemed strange without Bobby Robson but most of the World Cup team was there. Peter Shilton had retired and Chris Woods took his place in goal. Lee Dixon was at full back and John Barnes was preferred to Chris Waddle. I was really pleased that Gary Lineker was made captain, and he managed to score the only goal just on the stroke of half time. Although our performance wasn't brilliant we won, and that's important for any new manager.

Then on the 17th October we played in the European Championship against Poland. Again, the team was mainly made up of the old guys and we won 2–0 with goals from Gary Lineker with a 39th minute penalty and Peter Beardsley a minute before time. After scoring, Gary was taken off with an awful head injury that needed eight stitches.

*Four against one's not fair*

The match where we really needed to get a result was against the Republic of Ireland in Dublin on the 14th November. I was really gutted to be told that I wasn't going to play but it's the manager who picks the team and he preferred a combination of Gordon Cowans and Steve McMahon. Chris would have played in this match but unfortunately was injured the day before. It's never going to be easy playing against Ireland, particularly when they're at home and Jack Charlton has somehow merged a load of good club players into a great national team who play like men possessed. David Platt put us ahead after sixty-seven minutes but there was an inevitability about Tony Cascarino's equaliser. At the end of the day we were quite pleased to get away with the 1–1 draw.

I was back once more for the friendly against Cameroon on the 6th February and was also pleased to be playing alongside Bryan Robson again. Gary Pallister came on as a sub for him after seventy minutes and Steve Hodge replaced me after

*Omam Biyik in World Cup action against Argentina. Happier days for Cameroon*

*Here I am telling Graham Taylor about my fishing exploits*

sixty-seven minutes. The move towards the future was Nigel Clough on the bench although he didn't get a game. However, we won fairly easily, 2–0, Gary Lineker scoring both goals. Cameroon were simply not the same side that we'd met in the World Cup. Roger Milla pulled out after a financial dispute, and they obviously didn't like the English winter and didn't really want to play.

I wasn't to know it then, but that was the end of my international appearances for the season. I wasn't chosen for the match against the Republic of Ireland in the European Championships at Wembley on the 27th March and I had to pull out of the trip to Turkey due to the recurrence of my groin injury. I was never going to play against Russia on the 21st May because of the Cup Final, and I eventually watched the game against Argentina from my hospital bed.

However, England lost none of the matches and it was interesting to see from the Argentina game how much the English style, formation and players had changed over just eight months. David Batty, Geoff Thomas, Alan Smith, Lee Sharpe, Dennis Wise, Nigel Clough – Graham Taylor was clearly picking his own team on his own terms. Every manager has to do that if he's to be judged by results and to be still undefeated after eleven games in charge (including narrow wins against Australia and New Zealand) meant he was doing a good job. I just hope that I'll be back playing for England in the not too distant future, and that when I finally recover from my injury, wherever I may be playing, Mr Taylor won't forget me.

# 13
## Promotion and play-offs

While Derby and Sunderland sadly looked forward to Second Division football this season, West Ham, Oldham and Sheffield Wednesday automatically moved up. The Hammers had looked certainties to go up since last Christmas and most players have always regarded them as a First Division side. Oldham were terribly unlucky last year but this time around Joe Royle's boys (without Cup disturbances) made it as Champions. Earl Barrett also made it into the England team, making his debut against New Zealand. Although he didn't have a great match, I'm sure he'll be back when he's had more experience at top level. David Hirst also made his England debut against Australia and I think Sheffield Wednesday will do really well in the top flight next year. I'd love to be there when they play Villa!

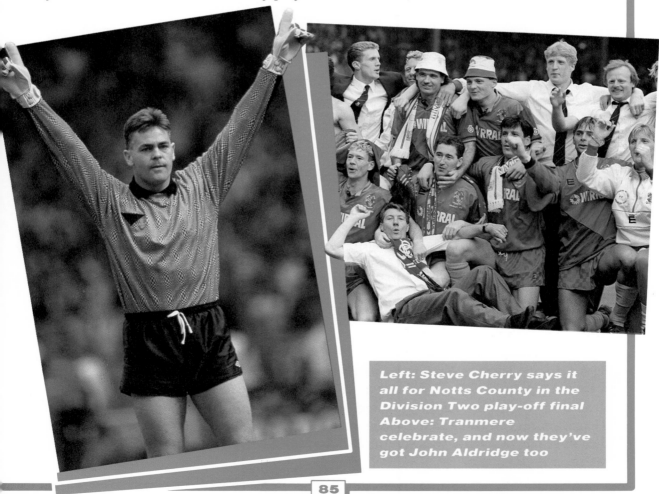

*Left: Steve Cherry says it all for Notts County in the Division Two play-off final*
*Above: Tranmere celebrate, and now they've got John Aldridge too*

**Wes Saunders shows what it's like to score at Wembley**

Notts County, quite deservedly, joined them from the play-offs. They'd finished 10 points ahead of their opponents, Brighton, and had played good football all year (particularly against us, as I have said before). Love or hate the play-offs, they do add a bit of drama to the end of the season. Neil Warnock has done brilliantly with County, taking them from third from bottom in the Third to the First Division in two seasons. Southend United, Cambridge United (what a good job John Beck did with them) and Grimsby Town got the automatic places while Tranmere Rovers who'd unluckily missed out last year got the play-off place with a 1–0 extra time win against Bolton.

As a Geordie, I was well pleased when Hartlepool and Darlington moved up from the Fourth, together with Stockport and Peterborough United. Darlington won the Conference only a year before, then promptly lost Brian Little, their manager – the price of success?!

Torquay won the play-off against Blackpool in less happy circumstances – on penalties 5–4. It's really no way to settle the outcome of a season. Why not give the match to the team with most corners, which at least encourages attacking football? Still Wes Saunders (another ex-Newcastle player) was the successful captain and got two goals in the final if you count his penalty in the shoot-out.

Barnet came up into the league although that success was tinged with sadness when Kevin Durham, their 29-year-old midfielder, died on holiday. It really makes you feel less sorry for yourself when you hear news like that.

Ninety-three teams in the league for 1991–92. Who'll be up, who'll be down, who'll be the successes, who'll be the disappointments? It's questions like that to which no one knows the answers that make football so fascinating. Playing or not playing, I can hardly wait for August.

# 14

## The things they say

Gazza, being a modest fellow, declined to have anything to do with this chapter (but nevertheless read it with interest!) and it has been provided by Mel Stein.

### Chris Waddle

*Fellow Geordie Chris Waddle had a fantastic year with Marseille, winning the French Championship and just missing out in the Final of the European Cup. Interestingly that match went to penalties but Chris declined to take one – perhaps remembering his disappointment in the World Cup semi-final against West Germany.*

*His opinion of Gazza? 'Great to have on your side. Paul enjoys playing football with a smile. I think a move to Italy, if he makes it, will suit him because of the emphasis on skill.'*

### Tony Dorigo

*Ex-Chelsea star Tony Dorigo is fighting hard to make the England full-back place his own. A £1 million-plus transfer to Leeds will do nothing to hinder that ambition.*

*On Gazza, Dorigo has this to say: 'He can turn a game with his magic. He's a very special player. He's also a total nut case; I roomed with him once on an England trip. One night is enough for a lifetime.'*

What was that Bobby Robson said?

## Steve McMahon

Liverpool and England midfield battler, Steve McMahon's career, like Gazza's, has been affected by injury. Steve is now looking forward to a full recovery and a great season with the Reds back in Europe and under new management at Anfield.

His view of Gazza's year. 'Paul, and Gary Lineker, have held Spurs together. In addition, Gazza is definitely the most appealing player to watch in England. His skill level is so high. And being so young, he's still got room to improve.'

## Glen Roeder

When it comes to skill and experience there are so few players around in the Glen Roeder class. Now with Watford, Glen knew Paul at Newcastle where the tall defender spent several happy seasons.

He remenbers a young Gazza. 'Paul could be absolutely brilliant or very frustrating. In those days he'd always have to go for the most difficult option, but everybody still loved playing alongside him.'

## Paul Stephenson

A team mate of Paul's when they were both Arthur Cox's 'babes', Paul Stephenson nearly bounced back to the First Division with Millwall, just losing out in the play-offs to Brighton.

Does he remember anything special about the young Gazza? 'I can't think of one of the stories about him when we were playing together that would be printable! But I do know what a fantastic job he's done for Spurs. Also, it must be said, he's been brilliant in handling a press that only seems interested in his private life.'

## Ian Bogie

Ex-Newcastle, and now with Preston (but for how long?), Ian Bogie sufferd a broken ankle last season which cut short a return to form. Many thought he would fill the gap in the Newcastle team created when Gazza moved south, but things didn't quite work out for him.

Bogie has a firm opinion on Gazza. 'He's definitely one of the top few players in the world today. And if he goes to play abroad, he'll only get better!'

## Steve Watson

Steve Watson is a name to watch for the future. A find-of-the-season as far as Newcastle are concerned, he's expected to improve even more under the guidance of new Magpies manager Ossie Ardiles

Does the young Watson admire 'old man' Gazza? 'At a time when too many people take the game far too seriously Paul is good for the fans and for football generally. He deserves a medal for keeping his temper with the media who really have treated him badly at times.'

## Nigel Spackman

Nigel Spackman plays his football north of the border with Rangers, and completed a fantastic season as the Glasgow side edged out Aberdeen for the Premier League title on the last day of the season.

He has an interesting view of Gazza. 'Gazza's displays in the World Cup were even more remarkable when one remembers how few international matches he had played before being thrown in at the deep end. The European Championships in 1992 should provide another grand stage for him and his skills.'

## Paul Parker

England defender Paul Parker overcame injury to regain a place in the England team and to push Queen's Park Rangers up the league in 1990/91 following a dreadful start to the season.

On the subject of Gazza, Parker is very direct! 'Off the field he can drive you mad. He never shuts up. On the field? He's just brilliant.'

## Gudni Bergsson

Icelandic international, and Tottenham team-mate, Gudni Bergsson had a disappointing year by his high standards. But he's not the kind of player to stay down for long; a new season will mean a new challenge for him.

Gudni has seen the pressure on Paul at close range. 'I don't think the public have any idea just how intense the pressure can be on Gazza, but he's done himself proud in coping with it. Although a move abroad may benefit Paul, the game in England will be the loser.'

## Neil McDonald

*Starring in a revitalised, but still erratic, Everton side, Neil McDonald played alongside Gazza in Newcastle. Having played both with and against Gazza gives Neil an interesting view of the man.*

*He explains. 'When you're with him the managers want you to give the ball to Gazza; when you're against him the managers concentrate on stopping him. I heard one say that to stop Gazza was to win the match.'*

## Paul Harding

*Gazza remembers Paul Harding, the Notts County midfielder, for the marking job he did on the Spurs star in the sixth round FA Cup tie. County fans are more likely to remember him for the goal he scored that won the play-off final and a place in the First Division.*

*Harding recalls Gazza from that Cup match. 'I knew he wouldn't like being marked man-to-man, and it's not a job I particularly enjoy either. But when you're playing against somebody who I think is the best player in the world, you've got to try something a bit special. Generally I was pleased with my performance and would like another match against Gazza; even better, I'd like to play in the same team as him.'*

## Peter Beardsley

*Peter Beardsley left Newcastle about the same time as Chris Waddle; their departure only increased Gazza's determination to leave the North East. Beardsley went to Liverpool and became a regular for the club and his country. He's a great fighter, and an inspiration to youngsters everywhere.*

*About Gazza, 'Beardo' explains: 'Everybody in the game knows him for his sense of fun; we just accept him for what he is, something the media seem unable to do. I think he's coped fantastically with all the pressure over the last couple of years.'*

## Paul Stewart

Paul Stewart joined Spurs at the same time as Gazza and has become the Geordie lad's closest friend at the club. Stewart's own time at Spurs hasn't been without its ups and downs, but the crowd have really accepted him now he's settled into a regular place in Terry Venables' side.

He thinks the injury to Gascoigne is a major blow, but one that Paul can get over. 'He'll be back, because that's the sort of player he is... a battler. The Final showed that Spurs are not a one-man team, but let's be honest, many fans both at home and away only came to see us because Gazza's name was on the team sheet.'

## Gary Mabbutt

Gary Mabbutt, team captain over the last year, has been an inspiration to the side. He's a quiet man off the pitch, getting on with his job. But when he does talk people listen, because he doesn't speak unless he has something to say.

Like most people in the game, Mabbutt has a funny story about Gazza. 'When Paul found out I was diabetic he asked how many times a day I had to inject myself. I told him four times a day for the rest of my life. His reply? "I bet you can't wait to die!"'

## Paul Davis

Paul Davis, one of the quiet men in the Arsenal side has served his club magnificently. With two Championship medals already won, he'll be relishing the challenge of Europe this year, and hoping to win a few more England caps.

For Davis, Gazza is an automatic chioce for a World XI. 'I'd nominate him immediately, and I wouldn't worry about his temperament. Although he has had a few tussles on the field (some with me) over the years he's a very sporting player at heart and doesn't mean any harm.'

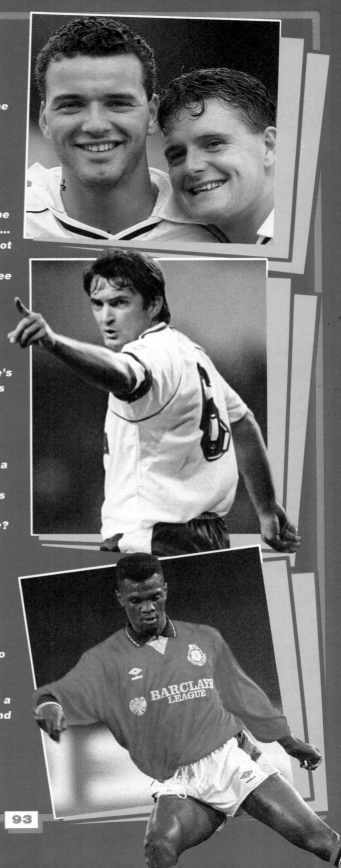

## Arthur Cox

Arthur Cox managed Gazza during the important early years of his career at Newcastle United. Cox then moved to Derby County where, sadly, with limited means, he has been unable so far to work his magic spell.

Cox's verdict on his star 'babe' is very illuminating. 'I quickly saw in him a great enthusiasm for the game. Also he's got incredible determination to win. You have to build on these characteristics. As for his "problems" with the media; I think he'll get on better when he learns to enjoy the attention more.'

## Colin Suggett

Colin Suggett was Newcastle Youth team coach before having a brief spell in charge of the First XI. He has watched his young star develop and mature since leaving the North East.

Suggett has this to say about Gazza. 'There are very few players who can turn a match with just a couple of pieces of brilliance. I'd put him in the same class as Best, Law and Charlton... and there are few players around who deserve that much respect.'

## Bobby Robson

Former England manager Bobby Robson once described Gazza as 'daft as a brush', and the Press seemed surprised at the comment! Robson does seem to have a soft spot for Paul, although this clearly never influenced his decisions in selecting (or not) Gazza for his England team.

Robson, who now manages PSV Eindhoven, this year's Dutch champions, knows a great deal about the Continental game. 'I think it would be sad if Paul did go abroad, but you can't pretend that he wouldn't benefit from such a move. Wherever he goes he'll succeed, providing he gets enough rest and retains his enthusiasm for the game.'

## Terry Venables

Spurs manager over the past couple of seasons, Terry Venables has had an enormous influence on both Gazza's game and his life outside football. Constantly in the news himself, Venables knows all about the pressures on the top names.

On the subject of Gazza, 'El Tel' has this to say. 'There are definitely two sides to Gazza. He can get very angry. But no sooner has he exploded then he wants to put matters right, because he is very sensitive and doesn't wish to hurt anybody. Basically he's very likeable.'

# 15

# My Hero of the Year

I know that I will get over my injury but the same cannot be said for Ray Kennedy, the ex-Arsenal, Liverpool and Swansea star who will be battling against Parkinson's disease for the rest of his life.

His career was quite exceptional, winning the double while at Arsenal and going on to win a host of trophies, including two European Cup medals, while with the Anfield side.

Right now he needs all the help he can get as he struggles, not only to live with his own problems but to promote a campaign to win funds for research into the crippling disease. I wish him all the best – he's an example to us all.

Ray Kennedy, then and now – a true Geordie hero